The People's Retirement Handbook

THE

People's Retirement Handbook

INSIDER TIPS YOU MAY NOT HEAR FROM OTHER FINANCIAL PLANNERS

Joel Johnson

BIG
MAN
PUBLISHING

THE PEOPLE'S RETIREMENT HANDBOOK

Essential Insider Tips You May Not Hear
from Other Financial Planners

ISBN   978-1-5445-0111-6 *Paperback*

978-1-5445-0112-3 *Ebook*

This book is dedicated to my parents, Fred and Elsie Johnson, for their example of how to live a life of sacrifice and service to others.

Also, to my wonderful wife, Wendy. Our home and children would not be the same without you.

Finally, to all my team members at Johnson Brunetti, my friends at Advisors Excel, and the many mentors, coaches, and coworkers who have shaped my life.

Contents

Regulatory Matters

IMPORTANT—READ THIS FIRST

This book is my opinion, based on my professional and personal observations.

I've observed friends and acquaintances who were wealthy, others who never seemed to get ahead, and still others who were miserable.

The ideas and statements in this book are not absolutes; they do not apply to all who are wealthy or all who are struggling financially.

I am the majority owner in an investment advisory firm registered with the Securities and Exchange Commission, as well as the majority owner of an insurance agency.

Nothing in this book is a recommendation of an investment or a promise of future results. This book's goal is to get you thinking about your thinking and behavior around money.

I want this book to help people improve their relationship with their finances. It is clearly not intended to recommend investment products or strategies, because as you well know, recommendations need to be customized to the individual's needs.

Introduction

When I was twenty-seven, I transitioned to the field of financial planning in 1989. My career move was partly a practical decision; my wife, Wendy, and I had been married for two years, and we were preparing to have a family. I wanted to settle on a career with solid prospects and move on from the entertainment business, which is highly volatile and unpredictable.

I believe financial planning was always in my blood. I knew the transition was a wise move professionally, but the truth was that I had always been interested in investments. I had always enjoyed reading books and articles on the subject, and I had developed a keen interest in the subject over the years. Eventually, I sat for the Series 7 examination, a challenging test that everyone wishing to sell securities must take. Only about 65% of the people who take it pass the first time.* Passing allowed me to work with a small brokerage firm in Florida.

Finance is an emotionally charged subject, and the way people handle money is deeply personal. They consult financial planners because they want to feel a sense of security and to relax, knowing that their investments are in good hands. They may arrive in their financial planner's office nursing deep, unspoken fears. Yet, the training I received as a registered representative at a brokerage firm never addressed how I should respond to those fears. Little did I know how much I would discover along my journey.

By industry standards, the training I received was excellent, but it consisted entirely of hard facts and practical advice. I always felt that some key element was missing. I already knew plenty about stocks and bonds, but no one had taught me how to tackle the disorientation that occurs in people who are fearful about their future or their family's future. I wanted to learn what to do when someone walks into the office seeking not only advice but also reassurance.

I believe that a financial planner who offers only analysis-based advice is doing half the job. People are scared when

---

* "The Series 7 Exam: What to Expect and How to Prepare," *Wall Street Prep*, 2018, www.wallstreetprep.com/knowledge/a-complete-guide-to-the-series-7-exam/

it comes to money. My training left me unprepared to deal with the deep fears that financial questions often create and to nurture the confidence that people needed to feel in order to make good decisions. A good financial planner will guide families toward enjoying their lives, not being fearful of the lack of money to fulfill their dreams.

Too often, the financial services industry does a poor job of serving people. It's full of math whizzes who want to trade stocks, bonds, and currencies around the world. It's full of analysts who can take a clinical stance based on algorithmic calculations. Generally speaking, it's not an industry that serves ordinary people who want to raise their children, retire, provide for a spouse after their death, and have the finances to handle any eventuality that might occur in their old age.

Very quickly, I decided that I didn't want to be that type of financial planner. I wanted to be someone who understood the emotions of clients and supported them based on their real—sometimes unspoken—priorities.

THE QUESTION BENEATH THE QUESTION

If you've ever experienced fear, in any circumstance, you understand that it doesn't respond to logic. Right now, think of something that scares you. Let's say you're afraid of heights. No matter how much someone tells you that the bridge won't collapse or the building has been here for fifty years, it doesn't make your fear go away. You don't need logic; it doesn't help. Now imagine that you have an investment portfolio, the economy is in trouble, the news is filled with negative outlooks on the economy, and your investments are down 20 percent. This might be perfectly normal, but if you're in the grip of fear, you may succumb to the temptation to act unwisely. You could lose a lot of money, all because you act from a place of panic. This is why it is imperative that your financial planner understands your questions beneath your questions.

What does this look like? Let me provide an example. In my current practice, typical clients might be a sixty-year-old couple. They are five years away from retirement, and they want to know whether or not they have enough money.

The way they present their question may imply that they want a mathematical answer. "Joel, do we have enough to retire?" Based on an agreed rate of spending, we can do some calculations, figure out a rate of return, and conclude that they'll be fine. Or we might conclude that it's too soon for them to retire and that they should work for a few more years.

At some deep level, however, whatever answer we come to will be insufficient. Why? Because what they're really saying is that they're approaching a major transition in their lives and are not sure how it will feel. They may not even know how to admit to the uncertainty and anxiety that are dominating their thinking. Many financial planners can tell them how they should manage their money. What they really need is someone to let them know if they're on the right track.

The point is this: what clients say they want and what they actually need may be very different. Maybe you can relate to one couple I recently started working with. Their initial question was whether or not they could retire in two years. Beneath that question, however, I noticed some major anxieties. One of their children is addicted to drugs, and they feel heartbroken and powerless. Additionally, they have a family history of Alzheimer's disease and feel scared that one or both of them will develop the disease.

In working with this couple, I certainly need to consider the financial component to their question. If one member of the couple *does* succumb to Alzheimer's, there will be financial repercussions. However, I also need to do my best to prepare them to enter an uncertain phase of their lives.

YOUR RETIREMENT

This book is for you, whether you are planning your

retirement or are already retired. You might have retired some years ago and now want to make sure that you're making the right choices with your money. Perhaps your goal is to make your investments sound. You're comfortable in the retirement phase of your life, and your interest in connecting with a financial planner comes from a desire to check that you're maximizing the value of your capital and not making any mistakes you might come to regret.

It's possible that you feel unsure how much you can support your children or grandchildren. Perhaps you're concerned that future generations of your family, especially those who are in the early years of adulthood today, won't have the same opportunities as you did when you were growing up. You want to help your grandchildren but don't want to deprive them of the lessons you learned by starting with nothing.

You may be just now on the cusp of retirement. In that case, you're probably caught up in the drama of big life changes, and your immediate concern is that the process will flow smoothly. You may need to discuss the progress of your investments and the process of turning your assets into a reliable income stream while sheltering them from taxes. You want somebody to be straight with you so that you don't make a major error and walk into retirement before you're ready.

You may have only just recovered from the cost of educating your own children. To catch up from these expenses, you might be considering somewhat risky investments in order to build retirement quickly. But let's be clear: you can't afford to take a big hit to your savings from a stock market downturn. You may not have the time to recover.

If any of these situations describes you, the right financial advisor can guide you toward an investment mix that seeks not to expose you to too much risk. The more time you have to get your finances in order, the more likely you will be able to position yourself for a strong retirement.

My grandparents lived through the Great Depression, an experience that forever shaped their relationship with money. Now members of the baby boomer generation who grew up in the prosperous 1950s and 1960s are entering retirement. They may have very different attitudes toward money than my grandparents did.

If you grew up in poverty, you may be more cautious with money than someone who grew up wealthy. My wife grew up in a family where prosperity was viewed with suspicion. Even today, she remains uncomfortable with any outward displays of success. I grew up in a family where my parents did charity and church work. Money was a matter of faith. They trusted that God would provide and thus were not focused on what they didn't have. As you can imagine, my wife and I entered into marriage with very different financial philosophies. This is common among couples, and it doesn't necessarily go away when you retire.

As financial advisors, it's our job to understand the character of our clients and seek to set them up for success. We need to understand why certain behavior is common in times of stress. Our job is to help clients avoid sabotaging their own efforts and acting against their own best interests.

In recent years, this industry, in some circles, has been reduced to a software program, but I do not believe in any cookie-cutter approach to financial planning. Today, anyone can feed a series of numbers into a computer, and a "robo-advisor" will tell them how to invest their savings. The irony is that these programs are generally written by young coders who have no experience managing their own money. They cannot and do not take into account the individual needs of each person, nor can they anticipate the stress that will likely rise because of the wrong decisions or circumstances beyond the investor's control.

Financial planning is not unlike other aspects of life. Even when we know what we *should* do, it's not always easy to stick to our good intentions. I like ice cream, and I know that I should eat less of it. How can I cut down my ice cream consumption? The easiest way is not to keep it in the house. By doing that, I set up my environment for success. When we set up a client's financial plan, we want to set them up for success. We want to prevent them from making mistakes by—ideally—making those mistakes a little harder to make.

OUR APPROACH TO WORKING WITH OUR CLIENTS

As you've probably guessed by now, our firm is not interested in running the numbers and dishing out generic advice. Sometimes a prospective client will walk into the office to meet us for the first time, plop their financial statements and tax returns on the desk, and ask how we can help them.

Our first response is to set the documents aside and spend some time getting to know them. Before we can offer them valuable advice, we need to know what has made them financially successful. We also need to know about times when they've been less successful, and how those times may have influenced their financial philosophy.

Imagine going to a doctor who is perfectly educated, with qualifications from one of the top schools in the country, but who doesn't take the time to get to know you or understand your situation. How would you feel about that experience? Now imagine a doctor who is qualified, can't boast quite such impressive credentials, but does take the time to listen to your concerns and reassure you. The latter prioritizes the relationship, and it's likely you will feel the difference.

We want all our clients to feel that difference in our office. We want to build a relationship with each and every client. We need to understand their goals, their dreams, and their fears. We ask them questions directly. In times of stock market volatility, a person's fears will have a huge influence on how they respond and behave. Remember, whether they verbalize it or not, deep down inside many people are scared. These feelings influence the financial plan we design for them.

Wisdom is what our clients can tap into through us. When I sit down with clients who are sixty years old, I can draw on the experience of previous clients who are seventy-five or eighty and use that experience to provide our younger clients with wisdom so they can anticipate challenges over two decades. This dynamic gives our clients a lot of peace of mind.

WHAT WILL YOU FIND IN THIS BOOK?

You may be wondering how this book can help you. As I hope you can already see, I believe you are an individual with your own unique needs. While I can't cover every possible eventuality in these pages, my hope is that you'll recognize yourself and your situation in the stories included here. With a little reflection, you should be able to get a sense of your personal tendencies and begin to understand your strengths and weaknesses.

You should also find some practical advice that you can use as a framework for understanding the choices facing you as you contemplate your own retirement. This book alone may not be enough to answer every question you have about planning your finances, but it should provide you with knowledge and tools that you did not have before.

This book will offer practical advice. Again, this book can't possibly address deep details on taxes, specific investment products, capital markets, and worldwide economics, but you will find information about different financial products and the circumstances in which each can be valuable. What I will not be doing is telling you precisely what stocks to buy or sell. That's a question you can only answer in collaboration with a trustworthy financial planner.

Really, this book is designed to give you perspective— perspective you probably will not get from others in the financial advice industry.

Ultimately, I hope you'll close this book with the feeling

that with the right support, you can meet your monetary challenges and feel good about your financial future. Even if you've been through negative experiences in the past with financial consultants, there are good people in this profession who will tell you the truth and serve you with integrity.

PART I

A Peek behind the Curtain

RUNNING AN INVESTMENT FIRM

I am the CEO of a retirement planning and investment firm.

You might think that what we do as financial planners is sell financial products. We don't see it that way. The products themselves—stocks, bonds, mutual funds, annuities—are merely tools to help people reach their goals. Sadly, many companies and individuals in our industry take a different view.

We can't give sound financial advice without understanding the specific fears and dreams of our clients. Of course, it's important that we have a solid practical knowledge of financial planning and different investment strategies, but the most important thing is to understand how our clients think and feel. This allows us to use the tools that best protect them from decisions that could hurt them.

We aim to combine familiarity with our clients' emotions with an intimate understanding of the nuances of various financial products. This is the only way we can attempt to marry the strategies and products to the people who need them. We want to know which approach will work best for each individual client; we strive to give them full confidence in their retirement planning.

We don't see ourselves as technicians. In our industry, a technician is someone who analyzes financial markets without considering the human element or the fundamentals of the companies they invest in. Technicians don't pay attention to human emotions; they're removed from the complex psychology of working with people. Instead, they are usually absorbed in the minute movements of financial markets.

Technicians are similar to auto mechanics. Mechanics don't consider the emotions of the human who will drive the car they are fixing; they're focused on the mechanical qualities of the car. Technicians may possess fantastic knowledge about financial products, but they apply them without a real understanding of the individual investor. We take the opposite approach. We possess plentiful practical knowledge, but our main focus is on crafting financial plans to suit individual clients and families—plans they can stick to when their emotions are screaming at them to change course.

FROM IDEA TO SIGNIFICANCE

Nancy Brunetti and I founded our company in 2003. From the beginning, we knew that we wanted to serve a broad cross-section of society. We treat everyone with respect, regardless of how much money they have. Indeed, I like to think that we take care of clients the way we would take care of our own parents. We both came from middle-class families, and we decided we wanted to build a company to serve not only the wealthy but also people like our parents. I have observed that most companies in the financial services industry spend much of their time chasing a few wealthy clients. I have also observed that many stockbrokers who give financial advice don't have much money themselves.

We wanted people to feel comfortable with us, knowing that we'll try to do the right thing for them and their money. Our determination to treat everyone with respect and to do what's right for the people in our care has made us extremely successful. We've grown a great deal since 2003, yet we've always held on to those founding ideas.

From the company's founding, Nancy and I were co-CEOs. We leveraged our distinct leadership styles to build the company together, as a team effort. I like to focus on creating a vision for the business and delegating responsibility to a management team, which means allowing them to experiment—and possibly fail. I prefer to give management authority and allow them to run their own business units. Nancy's style is to dig into the details of the company and get involved in every activity. We were a great combination to build a firm that could serve several thousand families.

From the beginning, the company was very busy. I played the role of financial advisor, while Nancy managed operations. Since then, we've grown from a company led by two people to a mature business with multiple leaders managing various departments. Eric Hogarth joined the company in 2007. He quickly became a rising star, and in 2012, the year after Nancy left, he became a partner.

When Nancy's children graduated high school, she became an empty nester. She had always dreamed of moving to Florida, where she owned numerous rental properties, and we decided it was the perfect time for me to buy out her interest at a fair price. Nancy and her husband, Todd, moved to Florida, and she became a successful consultant and realized her dream.

Despite the changes Johnson Brunetti has been through

over the years, we always strive to attain the same goal. We want to remove the *fear* from a client's financial future and give them *confidence* in what lies ahead. That ambition is posted in every conference room where we meet with clients. Many people, when they sit down with us for the first time, point to the plaque and say, "That's what I want."

WHAT DRIVES BEHAVIOR?

Tragically, most advisors don't know what drives their clients.

We ask a lot of questions about the events and experiences that have shaped the lives of our clients.

Sometimes we have the privilege of asking questions that invite clients to reveal their vulnerabilities. For example, we might ask:

- Did you have a traumatic experience growing up?
- Did you lose a parent or sibling? How did that affect you?
- Did you ever experience a situation where your parents went bankrupt, or were you so affluent that you felt separate from the other kids at your school because you knew you had so much money that you never had to worry about anything?

- Were you so poor that you couldn't buy nice clothes and shoes like the other kids? Did you have to pay your own way through college, did you borrow the money, or did your parents pay?
- Did you have access to money to buy your first home, or did you struggle and work hard just to get by?
- What is the difference between the way you think about money and the way your spouse thinks about money?

These are questions that most advisors won't ask because they are scared of losing the client. These questions come long before we think about pensions, investments, and 401(k)s. They are crucial to understanding the hearts and minds of clients.

Most people, as they approach retirement, are unlikely to alter their worldview significantly. This means we need to build a financial plan that matches their existing tendencies and preferences. Otherwise, they may believe that it's not working and go against our advice. Knowing our clients is the basis of all our success.

OUR EVOLUTION

Initially, Johnson Brunetti started with fewer than a hundred clients. As of 2018, however, we've served several thousand households across New England and elsewhere. And we're still growing.

Even as we grow, however, we are as committed to every client who comes to us as we were in 2003. In fact, all of the leaders at the company are obsessed with honoring the relationship people have with us.

Along the way, we have developed strategies to avoid or solve several industry-wide problems. These are trends that we see throughout the industry that limit the effectiveness of financial advisors. What problems are we referring to? I'll explain below.

INDUSTRY NORM

- Financial advisors are trying to do too many things.

Too many financial advisors try to be generalists. They want to do everything, with the result that they don't do anything particularly well. By definition, a specialist chooses to excel in only one or two areas instead of being mediocre in many.

We specialize in working with families ten years before or after retirement. Our financial advisors concentrate on the client relationship, while support staff and other members on the team support them with quantitative analysis. This allows financial advisors to do what they do best, without sacrificing the quality of our technical expertise.

INDUSTRY NORM

- Too many people in the industry work on commission.

Working on commission is appropriate in some fields, but it can cause conflicts of interest. Financial advisors who earn 7 percent commission for selling one product, yet 4 percent commission for selling another, face an incentive to promote the product that earns them the most money. This is true whether it's best for the client or not. If there is a conflict, we endeavor to fully disclose it.

It is very difficult to completely remove all conflicts of interest from life. An orthopedic surgeon makes more replacing your knee than he or she does sending you to physical therapy. At some point, you are trusting the surgeon to do the right thing.

Removing conflicts isn't possible in every situation. Some products are designed by insurance companies to pay a commission. If there's ever a conflict of interest, we endeavor to disclose it to the client. When the client does better, we do better.

INDUSTRY NORM

- Financial advisors say they want to help as many people as possible, but they don't invest in new infrastructure or staff.

To serve as many people as possible, we attempt to educate families in the communities we serve. We do this by offering educational events at union halls, senior centers, and other companies. We participate in seminars and workshops open to the public.

In addition, we pay broadcasters to sponsor and appear on personal finance shows on television and on the radio where people, including nonclients, can ask me questions. Our aim is to provide education and get the word out about the services we offer. If people find value in what we do and want to talk to us further, they can make an appointment. We offer financial help to everyone, whether they are clients or not. In order to do this, I have a team that allows me to reach and help as many people as possible.

INDUSTRY NORM

- Companies struggle to manage growth, so they hit a wall.

As businesses grow, they become more complex—a phenomenon my business coach describes as the ceiling of complexity. When companies hit that ceiling, their business becomes more complex than they can manage, and they start going backward. As a result, the client suffers. The business faces the choice between dropping standards and disappointing clients, or stagnating.

There's nothing wrong with a business choosing to serve their existing clientele and not grow. However, I believe that anyone who has a lot of value to offer the world should figure out how to offer that value to as many people as possible. At Johnson Brunetti, we've built a leadership team to do that. This team consists of five people, each with a different area of responsibility. Every Monday morning, the team meets for as long as two hours to share relevant information and discuss strategy. This model enables us to continue growing and adding staff, without diminishing the quality of our services.

INDUSTRY NORM

- A client's financial well-being is tied to one financial advisor.

While we recognize the importance of serving clients as individuals, we also understand that making them dependent on a single financial advisor would be unwise. Imagine if the financial advisor they relied on were to get sick or move away. This would create problems with their account and potentially reduce their probability of financial success.

We prefer a different model. Each client comes under the auspices of a team of advisors—Eric, for example, works with a team of three people who actively meet with his clients. If he falls sick or needs to be out of the office for a while, the quality of service his clients receive remains consistent.

These points we have discussed give you a behind-the-scenes look into the financial services business.

MY EVOLVING ROLE

Now that we are a mature company, my primary responsibility within Johnson Brunetti is to do everything in my power so that the advice we provide is reliable and high quality, whichever advisor(s) a client works with. This means that I focus mainly on quality control, investments, and leadership: I guide and support our financial advisors so that they can serve clients more effectively.

With a client base of more than several thousand families, it would be grossly negligent of me to keep the company dependent on me. I may be one of the firm's founders, but I'm not irreplaceable. I want to do this for the rest of my life, but I also want to know that if something happens to me, our clients will be well served in my absence.

Although I have mostly stepped back from meeting with individual clients, I do work with a select few—mostly family members, friends, and members of my church—

and remain available for consultation and problem solving. This means meeting with Johnson Brunetti's financial advisors to strategize and offer advice. I make myself available when clients have concerns they want to share with me.

Nonetheless, it's important that I maintain some client relationships. You've probably heard stories of CEOs visiting department stores to understand the experience of customers and staff. They do this because they know that if they lose touch with the experience of the people who purchase their goods and services, they won't be able to provide effective leadership.

PRO BONO WORK

I've always believed that it's important to help as many people as possible, irrespective of their ability to pay. In practice, this means we do various types of pro bono work with people who are in difficult financial situations.

For example, I worked with a young couple from my church who had borrowed money to buy cars and gotten behind on house payments. All of a sudden, they found themselves struggling to pay their bills and unsure how to organize their finances to get back on their feet.

We also work with organizations such as Dress for Success

in Hartford, Connecticut, which helps single mothers and women who have gone through a divorce or other hardships and want to return to the workforce. The organization donates clothes for job interviews to the women they serve. We provide the women with basic financial advice so that they can make good decisions and lay the foundations for a successful transition.

We don't receive payment for these types of services, nor would we expect to. We provide them because we want everyone to have access to sound financial advice. Occasionally, we meet wealthy people who think that our commitment to serving everyone means that we lack the expertise to serve the wealthy. That's certainly not the case. We've been successful, we're doing well, and we feel it's our moral duty to share some of our success with people who are less fortunate.

STAYING FOCUSED

A friend of mine who owns a large business with millions of customers says, "As soon as you lose perspective on that one individual person and why they come to you, as soon as you start thinking in terms of the masses and how to get a thousand more customers, as soon as you lose perspective on the service you provide to the individual, you lose the ability to serve effectively." This sums up our approach at Johnson Brunetti. We believe that the way to accomplish our goals is to stay focused on each individual client relationship.

Just Tell Me What Time It Is!

WHAT IS FINANCIAL PLANNING?

Imagine this scenario. A married couple walks into the office. The husband is an engineer who designs jet engines for airplanes. His wife has spent most of their marriage working at home and managing the house while raising the kids. The husband is highly skilled in his professional life and used to feeling in control. His wife, on the other hand, is comfortable asking basic questions and isn't convinced that he understands their finances as well as he says he does. Due to his technical background, he is comfortable with complex concepts, but he struggles to explain them in simple terms. The spreadsheets he has created to reassure his wife only confuse and frustrate her.

She really just wants to know that they will be OK. To put it another way, she wants him to tell her what time it is, but he keeps telling her how to build a clock.

Dynamics like this are common in the office of a financial planner. Our role is to navigate them without making either spouse look bad, a task that requires some of the combined skillsets of both a psychologist and a marriage counselor.

You might think you already know what financial planning is. But I hope it is already clear that *good* financial planning is as much about people as it is about money. Our job as financial planners is to serve the people in our care.

This makes the job interesting, because people are more complicated than money. For example, many clients coming to see us for the first time feel overwhelmed. They may be wary of asking questions or looking stupid. Alternatively, as in our previous example, a married couple may have wildly differing ways of processing information and making decisions.

There's no doubt that the financial industry is full of complicated products. To confuse matters further, the industry is riddled with jargon. An unscrupulous financial planner could easily use that jargon to befuddle clients, with the intention of making themselves appear exceptionally smart. I aim to do the opposite with my clients.

Our job is to speak in simple terms, use analogies, and draw diagrams so that clients understand the concepts, strategies, and products we're discussing. Our meeting rooms and offices contain big whiteboards so we can illustrate those financial concepts and strategies. We do this so that clients understand their choices and make decisions that both we and they can stand by. After all, most people are visual and want to see things illustrated.

COMMON MISCONCEPTIONS ABOUT FINANCIAL PLANNING

In the modern United States, we live in a twenty-four-hour news cycle. Numerous channels—including CNBC, Fox Business, Bloomberg, and the BBC—offer financial advice. As if that weren't enough, people can Google anything they want. While it's great that we have access to so much information, clients sometimes develop mistaken ideas about financial planning from media outlets. As a result, they come to us with vague or mistaken notions.

For example, some people believe that financial planning is primarily about putting together a budget. It's not. Budgeting is important, and if you need to create a budget, there are many simple tools available on the internet, but it's not the point of financial planning, or of this book.

Other people come to us thinking we're credit counselors who will help them declare bankruptcy or get out of debt. As we discussed in the previous chapter, we do engage in pro bono work to help people work through their financial challenges. Credit counseling is about deciding which debts to default on, when to declare bankruptcy, and which creditors to call.

Another misconception is that it's better to work with two or three financial planners to diversify one's risk. Often, people think that they should hedge their bets so that if something goes wrong with financial planner A, financial planner B will have their back. This may sound sensible, but it may actually *increase* risk, because often the different financial planners do not communicate with one another. This sets you up for a scenario where something can go wrong. The exception to this is when you are in the midst of changing advisors. Sometimes there may be a short period when you are actually working with two people.

Finally, and most commonly, people approach us thinking that financial planning is only about choosing investments. They want us to tell them which stocks or mutual funds they should own. To be fair to them, many financial advisors act as though this is the entirety of their job, so it's not surprising that members of the public think the same way.

WHAT IS FINANCIAL PLANNING?

Everyone who wishes to become a certified financial planner must reach certain standards, decreed by the College for Financial Planning, in order to attain a Certified Financial Planner (CFP) designation. This rigorous qualification is similar to having a medical degree and being board certified. The "Board Certification" is a higher level of expertise. Specifically, according to the CFP Board, financial planners must have expertise in various areas. A complete and total financial plan consists of seven steps.

1. Understanding the client's personal and financial circumstances.
2. Identifying and selecting goals.
3. Analyzing the client's current course of action and potential alternative course(s) of action.
4. Developing the financial planning recommendation(s).
5. Presenting the financial planning recommendation(s).
6. Implementing the financial planning recommendations(s).
7. Monitoring progress and updating.

Good financial planners keep their focus on their relationship with the client, meaning that they view each step in the context of what's best for the individual with whom they're working.

Imagine you are an architect and you're building a house. Before you start, you need to create the plan. How do you do that? First, you ask questions to understand the needs of the client. You need to know how they want the house to look and what features or functions they desire.

Financial planning is similar. We endeavor to put together a structure that encompasses every part of a client's financial life. Additionally, we do things in an order that makes sense. If we were building a house, we wouldn't build the roof before the walls. In financial planning, we don't discuss investments before we understand the client's goals and design a plan after careful analysis. The investments must serve the plan.

A house needs solid walls, so the financial plans we create need to be solid and stable. If a client's income is uninsured, or if their life isn't insured for catastrophic health crises, the whole structure could come tumbling down. We begin with the end in mind, and then we design a plan that allows our clients to achieve their goals.

SIMPLICITY AND FLEXIBILITY

No client wants planning their financial future to be more complex than it needs to be. For this reason, we strive to keep all communication simple. We want people to know what they're signing up for. Some plans may be complex. Nonetheless, we aim to explain them as simply as possible. When clients leave our office, we know that they'll probably forget the details of their plan, but we want them to retain a clear picture of their overall goals. This will enable them to stick with the plan in the face of market fluctuations and economic difficulties.

Of course, we do have some flexibility. In this way, financial planning is unlike building a house. Once a house is complete, it's extremely difficult to make major changes such as relocating the walls. Good financial planning allows us to adjust our clients' plans to adapt to changes in the investment world, shifts in family dynamics, or alterations to their individual lives. Throughout the journey, our role is to put the client first and to always remember that our work only has meaning when it serves the goals of a real person.

In the next part of this book, we'll dive more deeply into how good financial planning can help you prepare for your retirement and what constitutes a good financial plan.

PART II

Your Retirement

IT'S ABOUT A LOT MORE THAN MONEY

You're going to live longer than your parents will. Maybe not you specifically, but if we have one hundred people your age in a room, most will live five to fifteen years longer than their parents. Think about it. Fifty years ago, when someone died at sixty-five we would say, "They lived a good life." Now if someone dies at sixty-five, we say, "They died so young."

There are other challenges today that didn't exist in previous generations. Someone who retires early—for example, at the age of sixty—might well have one or both parents still alive in their eighties. Simultaneously, members of younger generations tend to have children later in life, so a sixty-year-old retiree might still have kids in college or be paying off college expenses. This is why we are called the sandwich generation. We have kids needing financial help while parents may need support.

Many people saw their retirement savings drop in 2008 to 2010. According to global financial data, NBC News. com reported that between October 9, 2007 and March 5, 2009 the S&P went down 56.4%.[*]

For these reasons and many others, most people come to the process of planning their retirement with a lot of anxiety. They want to know whether they will be able to retire when they want to, and whether their money will last as long as they are alive. They worry about inflation and the state of the market. They fear that a spouse's investment strategy is incompatible with their own. Each of these fears is based on practical concerns, but the emotional charge attached to them can make it hard for people to take a deep breath and analyze their situation.

Even after we succeed in supporting them through these anxieties, they usually have others. When they trust that they will have enough money to retire comfortably, they want to know whether they will be able to provide for their loved ones, fund vacations, or provide for their spouse if they become disabled. Finally, they may want to know

---

[*] "11 Historic Bear Markets," *NBCNews.com,* http://www.nbcnews.com/id/37740147/ns/business-stocks_and_economy/t/historic-bear-markets/#.XD4utlxKiUk

whether they will have enough money to bequeath funds to a charitable organization whose work they believe in.

To sum up, their anxieties usually fall into three distinct categories:

- Will I have enough money to retire?
- Will I be able to care for loved ones?
- Will I be able to leave anything after I'm gone?

CRAFTING SPECIFIC GOALS

I'm a musician. I play guitar. If I want to improve, I need a specific goal to work toward—maybe a specific song to learn. I can hear that song in my mind and work on each individual part and thus succeed. However, if I restrict myself to vague goals, such as "becoming a great guitar player," I'm highly unlikely to have the desired outcome. I didn't quantify it, so I don't know when I'm making progress, which makes it difficult to stay motivated.

In a similar way, we can only create an effective financial plan when we understand the *specific* goals our clients want to attain. If someone says, "I want a successful retirement," many financial planners stop right there. You cannot achieve your goals until you know clearly what success looks like. The key is getting very clear answers to specific questions.

In our firm, once someone answers the question, "What are your goals for retirement?" we go deeper by asking, "What does that look like for you?"

If they say, "I want to travel," we may ask, "Where would you like to travel?"

They may answer, "I want to travel to Europe."

We would ask, "How often do you want to travel to Europe? Whom do you want to take with you? What do you want to do while you're there?"

I'm sure you get the idea. We drill down so that they have the opportunity to clarify exactly what a successful retirement looks like for them. When we do this, the emotional pull of the plan we eventually settle on is much greater. By getting specific, they develop a clear mental picture of their ideal retirement and subsequently buy into a plan that will take them there.

Once we have that clear picture, we can estimate the financial costs of achieving the dream. For example, we may work with a client who is already retired and wants to help their grandchildren go to college. To do this, we need to estimate how much college will cost by the time their grandchildren are ready to attend. Our aim is always to turn their dreams into reality, by first understanding the specifics of those dreams and then creating plans that will make those dreams come true.

INJECTING REALISM INTO PLANS

As much as we aim to satisfy the desires of our clients, sometimes we also need to rein them in. If someone comes to us with a dream of traveling to Europe six times a year to take winery tours, we need to build that dream into their planning scenario. Can they afford that? To this end, we need to calculate how far they are from retirement and what they can do with their money before then. If they have already retired, we must calculate that their basic income needs can be met before we look at vacations.

Some parents sacrifice their own retirement security by sending their children to colleges that are way too expensive. If they're not careful, they will spend their retirement living with their educated kids.

While unavoidable expenses include basic goods such as food and clothing, and we encourage every client to keep these in mind, the most significant expenses we encounter when creating a retirement plan are home and health. Statistically, a married couple in the United States can expect to spend at least $275,000 on medical expenses over the course of their retirement. It's essential that they prepare for these expenses. We'll discuss home expenses in depth later in this chapter, while we'll cover health in chapter 5.

We always explain to clients that they would be unwise to sacrifice their own financial well-being in an effort to help others. There must be a happy medium. The safety briefing on every commercial flight reminds passengers that in the event of an emergency, they must always attach their own oxygen mask before they help the person beside them. If they die trying to help someone else, that does no one any good.

Generally speaking, we work with two types of clients. There are those who find it difficult to clarify their specific dreams, and there are those who have many fond dreams they wish to accomplish. It's our job to help the latter hone their dreams into realistic, achievable goals. Sometimes part of our role is to provide practicality.

For example, we look at the state of a client's health. Someone with congestive heart failure and diabetes may not be in a position to help their infant grandchildren pay for college. Someone who is sixty but runs marathons may be able to look forward to at least three more decades of active, healthy life.

My mother, for example, is eighty-four years old. She

loves to travel and, due to my father's occupation, has been crisscrossing the world for many years. Unfortunately, she can no longer travel as much as she used to. When she catches a plane to visit her children and grandchildren, it takes her a day or two to recover. She can no longer walk the same distances as she could in her younger years.

There is always a risk that aging will lead to health restrictions, and this has to be factored into the plans we make. Clients who dream of traveling to Italy every year may be wise to plan on doing so early in their retirement, while they are still healthy and mobile.

In contrast to most financial planners, we work backward from our clients' ideal goals to reach a workable plan. We start with their vision of a perfect retirement, and only then do we look at the unavoidable expenses they will need to factor into their retirement.

In the rest of this chapter, we'll examine one of those unavoidable expenses, and also the subject of many people's retirement dreams: owning property. We'll discuss where to live, the advantages and disadvantages of renting over owning, and additional options such as owning multiple homes and living in a retirement village.

LOCATION, LOCATION, LOCATION

As mentioned in the previous section, home expenses are a major component of most people's retirement expenses. The majority of retirees will spend a significant amount of money on maintenance and upkeep. The biggest factor, however, may be the choice of where to live.

In the United States, the cost of renting or owning property varies wildly in different locations. Two cities located next to each other can show a tremendous cost differential. Even within a city, neighborhoods can vary drastically in cost. Where I live with my family in Connecticut, the costs of living are high. Housing, taxes, groceries, and fuel are higher in the northeast than in most of the United States. I could move to another part of the country, but I need to examine the aforementioned costs, as well as access to quality medical care, other services, and even the proximity to people who share my values. These are all factors that you will want to take into account when you choose where to live in retirement. Additionally, of course, you may have other reasons for preferring one area over another, such as proximity to children, grandchildren, or friends. For many of our clients, this trumps all other factors.

Often, when people move away from an area with which they are familiar, their health goes downhill. While I don't have medical research to back up this observation, I've seen it happen many times. Adult children may want their parents closer to them, so they can keep an eye on the parents as they age. This seems like a good idea, but it often precipitates a decline in the health of the parents. My own mom and dad recently moved back to Minneapolis, where they grew up, because they wanted to be close to the places they're most familiar with and the friends they knew when they were younger. Because they are comfortable there and close to friends, we don't anticipate a difficult adjustment. On the other hand, some retirees need to be careful about moving away from an area and people they are familiar with.

There are many lists available online that detail the best places to retire, but it's important to remember that where to live is a personal and subjective decision. If you're researching the best places to retire, it's helpful to know what matters most to you so you can make a decision in line with your priorities.

Where you make your home in retirement is part of your dream. It's vital that you understand what will bring you the greatest happiness and base your choice of location on an honest assessment of what will bring you fulfillment.

RENTING VERSUS OWNING

Traditional wisdom would have us believe that owning a home is an essential part of retirement. For some people this is no longer the case. Many retirees are choosing to sell their homes and rent instead—an option that clients never would have considered twenty-five years ago. Why are they doing this? There are several reasons.

The first is the flexibility of not owning a home. If they leave for a vacation, they don't need to worry about maintenance, mowing the lawn, or ensuring the water is shut off. They can simply lock the door and leave.

The second is cost. Believe it or not, it is often less expensive to rent a home than to own one. Property prices in the United States have increased rapidly over recent decades, but this trend is decelerating and may go into reverse, especially in the northeast, where most of our clients reside. Taxes, utilities, and heating are additional expenses. If you take into consideration the cost of upkeep, you may find that it's possible to sell your home, rent a property for the same amount of money, and still have funds left over for investment.

I've seen this dynamic in action. A married couple recently came to us for advice: the husband wanted to sell their home. "I've done some calculations," he said. "We have a mortgage that we're paying interest on, insurance, utility costs, and between $10,000 and $20,000 a year that we spend on upkeep such as yard work, painting, and unexpected expenses."

He had done the math and determined that it was possible to rent a place for the same amount he and his wife were spending on mortgage interest and upkeep. In addition, they would have money from the sale. Properly invested, those funds could pay their rent, enabling them to live in Florida for three months of the year without worrying about the state of their home.

Selling a home is a big decision, and at first his wife was reluctant. That's where they'd raised their children. They'd lived in the same home for many years, and she felt safe and secure there. Finally, however, she agreed. It's turned out to be an outstanding move for them. They live in a luxury apartment with a full complement of amenities, including a health club and pool. They don't need to take care of the beautiful grounds or fix broken appliances. Without the physical and emotional burdens of owning a home, they can travel wherever they want. Selling their home was a difficult decision, but now they are extremely happy.

Renting an apartment isn't right for everyone. It does mean giving up a degree of control, because renters don't own the piece of land their home is built on. If you like to work on your car in the backyard, or you want to create a big playground for your grandchildren, you may be out of luck. If you decide to rent, you will give up some control over what you can do with the property in exchange for greater flexibility.

WHAT ABOUT A MORTGAGE?

Those who own their home often believe that they should undoubtedly pay off their mortgage before retirement. Surprisingly, this isn't always the case. If you own a home worth $750,000 and have $250,000 remaining to pay on your mortgage, you could pay off that $250,000, put the money in the bank, or invest it. How should you decide? What are the primary criteria?

On a purely financial basis, you may be better off maintaining the mortgage and claiming the interest as a tax deductible. Investing what you would have used to pay down your mortgage may be a huge benefit. Think of the flexibility you have that you give up if you send that money to the bank to pay your mortgage.

On the other hand, you may have deep psychological reasons to pay off your mortgage. My parents decided that they didn't want to owe anything to anyone, no matter how financially beneficial it would have been for them to continue paying their mortgage into retirement. They prefer the peace of mind of not being in debt. They were raised that way. What should you do? That's a question only you can answer through careful thought. On paper, it probably makes sense to have a mortgage in retirement, but you must take into consideration your feelings about debt.

OWNING MULTIPLE HOMES IN RETIREMENT

Many people with a substantial income nurture a fantasy of owning multiple homes. Many of them own multiple homes. They imagine one primary house, where they live for most of the year, plus a vacation home on a lake or a cottage in the woods. Although this scenario is understandably attractive, it rarely makes good financial sense. The cost of owning a second home usually outweighs the benefits. Because of this, owning a second home should be based on what you want, not what makes sense on paper.

For example, perhaps you want to spend four months per year in Florida. It may seem like a good idea to purchase a second home, but there are significant downsides to consider. Do you want the hassle and extra cost of a second home? Do you want to handle the maintenance and yard work? Do you want to be responsible for finding someone to fix something if it breaks?

Also, what if you decide you would rather vacation in California one year? You will probably feel obligated to stay at your property in Florida instead. My wife, Wendy, and I don't own a second home. When the time comes for us to head off on vacation, we can go wherever we want. The idea of owning multiple properties seems exciting, which is why some people aspire to it. However, we know people who own an additional property, and many of them find the experience stressful and unpleasant, although they won't admit it.

LIVING IN A RETIREMENT COMMUNITY

Another option that many people find attractive is moving to a retirement community. My parents have a home in a beautiful retirement community in Southern California: it is their own independent home, but they have no responsibility for anything beyond the walls of that home. The community has numerous pools, a golf course, and a health center, with nutritionists available for appointments. It was the perfect combination of the benefits of owning a property and renting a property.

If you're currently in your fifties and thinking that you may want to move to a retirement community in a few years, now is a great time to start doing your research. When you're traveling or on vacation, take a drive through local retirement communities and check them out. When it's time to make a decision, you will already be well informed.

When it comes to preparing for and enjoying your retirement, there are many factors to take into consideration. Where you will live is one of the most important. Some of the factors determining your choice of home will be emotional, such as a desire to live near children, grandchildren, or friends. Some will be practical, such as cost and proximity to other services. How you weigh these factors relative to one another is up to you. It's the job of your financial advisor to understand your dreams, help you create a path to attain those dreams, and perhaps to provide a voice of reason so that you don't overreach.

You may be wondering exactly how a solid financial plan works and what difference it can make to your retirement. In the next chapter, I'll explain the difference between having a large sum of money and creating an income on which you can sustainably live—the key element of any good retirement plan.

Grandpa Pete's Retirement

IT'S ALL ABOUT INCOME

My grandpa Pete came over here on a boat from Norway when he was sixteen years old. He worked for a company in Minneapolis for thirty-five years. He retired and received a monthly pension check for life. If I walked out of my office, went to the software business down the hall or approached another random group of people, and asked them to tell me what retirement planning is, nine out of ten would say that it's about managing investments to grow their accounts.

On the other hand, if I had asked my grandfather the same question, he would have said retirement planning is about getting a pension that could cover all his monthly income needs for the rest of his life.

In previous generations, people understood this core concept of retirement. Yet, many people today think that planning for retirement is about saving a lump sum of money. That is too simplistic and many times sets one up for failure. Successful money management in retirement is actually about setting up investments that will provide consistent income on an ongoing basis. When you're planning your retirement, this should be top of mind.

Of course, we live in a very different world from the one my grandfather knew. In his generation, it was normal for people to work for the same company for twenty-five or thirty years. In exchange for that level of loyalty, the company set up and paid into a pension plan. When they retired, they received an income for the rest of their lives.

For various reasons, few companies offer pension plans nowadays, and those pensions that do exist are much less lucrative than the ones my grandfather knew. Many firms, especially public companies that trade on the stock exchange, have stopped offering pensions altogether. This is largely because Wall Street gets nervous when public companies carry liability on future pensions, seeing them as a large unknown on a balance sheet.

In a world of increasing longevity, companies don't know how long their employees will live. This means that offering pension plans is an expensive gamble. If companies underestimate their employees' life expectancy, they may end up paying out significant sums monthly for a lot longer than they funded for. To avoid that trap, a lot of companies have made the decision to terminate pension plans and instead pay out a lump sum, for employees to invest as they see fit. Others have switched to offering only 401(k) plans to limit their pension liabilities.

In other words, the responsibility for creating retirement income has shifted from companies to you. This is why it is so important to put together a solid plan that will generate consistent income for the duration of your retirement.

HOW TO START PLANNING YOUR INCOME

The quality of your cash flow in retirement will determine both your lifestyle and your chances of achieving your dreams. The more effectively you create a solid, predictable cash flow, the more you will reduce your levels of stress and anxiety.

The question is, how much do you need? This is complex. Many tools exist to help you calculate how much income you'll need to live on in retirement, but not all are reliable. One of the more problematic tools is the online calculator, a simple app designed to provide users with a basic budget. This may sound good, but free tools like these are too generic to offer tailored advice.

First of all, the app may be programmed by a twenty-five-year-old software engineer who doesn't have much money or any real understanding of how money works. Worse, someone in this situation won't ever have encountered the questions people in their fifties or sixties need to handle, nor accrued the wisdom that comes with decades of experience and mistakes.

As a consequence, online financial planning tools are usually superficial and provide only a static analysis. They won't tell you how to invest your money, which account you should withdraw from first, or which account you should keep as a last resort. In short, why would you seek advice about retirement from such a two-dimensional tool?

YOUR RETIREMENT INCOME PLAN

By contrast, the best financial planners create personalized retirement income analyses. To do this, we need to understand each individual's personal circumstances, including details that will never be captured by an online tool. The only thing our clients need to tell us is how much cash flow they want per month. We do all the work.

Here's an overview of the process. First, we figure out whether you will have enough money—based on your goals—to live comfortably for the rest of your life. In other words, we want to know whether you can you meet your goals without ever running out of money. Second, we determine the rate of return you will need on your investments to turn the life you want into reality.

This second step is crucial, because someone who can meet their goals with a 4 percent rate of return on their investments will pursue a very different strategy from someone who requires a return of 7 percent. To achieve a higher return, the latter will need to take some risk, and accept more volatility, in their investment portfolio.

A customized retirement income analysis identifies details like this but, more importantly, explores your attitudes toward risk, which will almost certainly be missed by online calculation tools. In my opinion, going through this analysis with a skilled financial advisor is best because it's both detailed and dynamic, providing the information we need to build a solid yet adaptable foundation, which we can later adjust to changing life circumstances. An online tool simply can't provide the same level of flexibility or subjective wisdom.

There are many different types of strategies and products to generate predictable retirement income, which can be used alone or in combination with one another, according to individual circumstances, expectations, and needs. Let's discuss some of them.

SOCIAL SECURITY

Social Security is a source of monthly income for Americans who have worked and paid into the Social Security system over the course of their lives. For those who haven't succeeded in saving money for retirement, Social Security may be their most significant source of income. Even people who have saved and invested enough money to carry them through retirement should take Social Security seriously. The average person's Social Security payment, if converted into a lump sum, would be worth somewhere in the region of $400,000 to $500,000. If you had that much money sitting in an account, you would certainly take it seriously.

When it comes to Social Security, the big question is whether it's a reliable source of income. People of my generation assume that we'd better have a good retirement plan in place or we'll be in big trouble, because we've seen the decline of Social Security during our lifetime.

It's possible this fear is exaggerated, simply because retired people and those close to retirement represent a huge voting bloc. For this reason, I think it is unlikely that either political party will significantly reduce Social Security for people over sixty years old. That said, benefits may be modified to maintain the solvency of the system. Younger people, such as my children, may see drastic reductions in future benefits by the time they reach retirement age.

When Social Security was designed, the government underestimated how long people would live. They based the entire system on the assumption that most people would be dead by the age of seventy. Today, many people are living into their eighties and nineties, placing unexpected strain on the system.

The definition of a Ponzi scheme is taking money from new investors to pay off previous investors. This is how Social Security actually works. Current workers' Social Security taxes are used to pay out the retirees who are receiving benefits right now. When we have more retirees than workers, we have a problem.

PENSIONS

There are several different types of pensions. Nowadays, very few people have a traditional pension plan, although this is the simplest option. If you do have one, you will receive a monthly check for the rest of your life on reaching retirement. A second style of pension, known as a "cash value pension plan," is an account into which money is contributed by the employer during a person's working life. If you leave the company, you can "roll over" that cash value to another plan.

Many people are understandably concerned that their pensions may suffer if the company they work for files for bankruptcy or terminates the plan due to liquidation. They want to know what will happen to their supposedly guaranteed income. The bad news is that a pension is a liability on a company's balance sheet. If a company goes into bankruptcy, the employees are some of the many creditors the company owes money to.

The good news is that the Pension Benefit Guaranty Corporation (PBGC) guarantees pensions up to a ceiling, in much the same way as the FDIC (Federal Deposit Insurance Corporation) does. I have a friend who is a pilot. When his airline went into bankruptcy, he lost a big chunk of his pension, but because of the PBGC, he will still get $3,000 per month. The amount you receive is based on your age when the company went into bankruptcy. Be warned, though. State and municipal employee plans and church pensions can opt out of paying into the government plan, so employees of churches and governments may not have any protection.

401(K) AND 403(B)

The 401(k) and the 403(b) are the two most common types of savings accounts for people planning their retirement. They work by automatically transferring money out of an employee's paycheck and into their savings account. In many cases, employers match some of the contribution made by the worker. The 401(k) is the most common and the most flexible: up to a prescribed limit, employees can even borrow money from their 401(k) for special needs, although we strongly recommend that people *never* borrow from their retirement savings.

These accounts are more protected than many people realize. Some employees fear that their employer can take away their 401(k), or that they will lose it if the company goes broke. Neither of these fears is justified. A 401(k) is a special account that is totally separate from company accounts, and that cannot be accessed by employers.

You can even set up a 401(k) if you work for yourself and want to create a retirement plan that has higher funding limits than traditional individual retirement accounts (IRAs).

TRADITIONAL IRAS AND ROTH IRAS

IRAs come in several forms that allow people to save for

retirement while saving on taxes. Here, we will explore two types.

If you have a traditional IRA, you will put money from your regular income into the plan, while simultaneously deducting the same amount from your taxes. If your income is too high, you may not get a tax deduction. When you decide to withdraw the money from your IRA, however, it will be subject to taxation. A Roth IRA works differently: money deposited in the account isn't eligible for a tax deduction, but it is tax-free when it is withdrawn during retirement.

In other words, these two different types, traditional versus Roth, give you a choice. You can save on taxes either when you deposit the money or during your retirement. Why does this matter? First, it is possible that taxes will increase in the future, making a Roth IRA more beneficial in the long term. If you utilize this option, you will receive back all the money you deposit, plus all the growth from subsequent investment, without tax.

On the other hand, there are some circumstances in which a traditional IRA is the smarter choice. If your tax bracket while you're working is higher than your tax bracket will be in your retirement, you may do better to save the tax immediately by using a traditional IRA.

Both traditional and Roth IRAs are subject to income

limits. If you earn more than a certain amount per year, money you deposit in a traditional IRA is no longer deductible, and you cannot deposit any money at all in a Roth IRA. The numbers change every few years, so I cannot put the limits in this book. Despite this drawback, however, many people find that an IRA is an extremely valuable tool for effective retirement planning.

Depending on your personal situation, you may be able to score a huge home run by converting a traditional IRA into a Roth IRA. The value of this move will vary based on how long you can leave the money in your account and the rate of return you receive, but it may be possible to pay taxes on a small amount of money today in order to avoid paying taxes on a large amount of money in future.

This is a complex maneuver and isn't suitable for everyone. But it's well worth exploring with a qualified financial planner.

HEALTH SAVINGS ACCOUNTS

A final note in this section. Health savings accounts are designed to cover medical expenses, either prior to retirement or afterward. Although they're not available to everyone, those who can use them can benefit enormously. Money placed in health savings accounts is tax deductible, and if it is used to pay for qualifying medical expenses, it can be withdrawn tax-free. Yes, the money enters the account before taxation and comes out tax-free. That's an excellent deal, especially for people approaching retirement.

DRAWING RETIREMENT INCOME

One of the trickiest questions people ask me is which retirement account they should draw money from first. Should they spread their withdrawals equally from each account, for example, or are they wiser to exhaust one account for expenses and avoid touching the others?

The answer to this question, like most questions in the realm of financial planning, depends on personal circumstances. The main factors you need to consider are the tax impact of the account over your lifetime, how much income you need, and the possible lost opportunity cost of drawing from a particular account.

For example, many people who need additional monthly income choose to leave their Social Security untouched so that it continues to accrue. To meet that income need, they spend from their 401(k). Broadly speaking, this aligns with the recommendations of the financial press.

Well, contrary to the wisdom of many publications, this may be the wrong choice. When they spend money from their 401(k), they lose the opportunity to earn interest on that money, which may not be a smart move. They may do better to use their Social Security funds earlier and allow their 401(k) to grow.

Additionally, you have a lot less control over Social Security than you do over your 401(k). You can't leave your Social Security to children, grandchildren, or charity. You cannot adjust withdrawals up or down. You may be draining an account you have a lot of control over just to leave Social Security alone. The problem is that you may die before you get all of your money out of Social Security.

You may have a pension, which you will also need to use strategically. Ideally, you will want to maximize the benefit of your pension in the context of your overall retirement plan. The primary decision is usually when you start to receive a pension: whether you take it immediately upon retirement or delay it as long as possible.

This is similar to Social Security. You may choose to delay receiving pension checks to let the money accrue. You may be in a position to take your pension as a lump sum instead of as monthly payments. The advantage of taking a lump sum is that you can roll it over, tax-free, into an IRA. This gives you more flexibility and control. For most people, this is the right way to go. The downside of doing this is that you accept responsibility for the investment risk on that lump sum. Should you invest unwisely, you could do worse than you would have by taking monthly payments but remember the issue of control. You have a lot more control and flexibility by rolling that pension over, tax-free, into an IRA and taking out monthly income.

Here's an option for those whose goal is monthly income. You can "buy" your own pension. Many people approaching retirement now create their own private pensions through the use of various insurance products, preferably with the help of a qualified financial planner. The more pensions go away, the more popular this strategy becomes. You can also retain control over this private pension if designed properly.

With all the different options we have discussed, the main principle to keep in mind is the opportunity cost of a given path. When you are about to withdraw from an account, ask yourself what you could earn with that money if you leave it in the account instead.

Complicating the picture still further is the issue of required minimum distribution. In the year that you turn seventy and a half, the IRS forces you to begin spending money from your retirement accounts. For some people, this can create a big tax problem. The good news is that with skillful planning, it's usually possible to reduce the potential lifetime tax liability of these required minimum distributions.

The bottom line is that different retirement plans offer different advantages and disadvantages. If you have multiple sources of retirement income—pension, Social Security, 401(k), IRA, or an investment or brokerage account—you have many opportunities to maximize your retirement income. Making the most of them requires careful thought and planning.

Just to summarize, when you create your retirement plan, your first priority should be the creation of stable, predictable retirement income. Remember this simple fact and you will be well on your way to shaping a satisfying retirement, and perhaps leaving something behind for your loved ones.

Even if you set up your income well, however, unexpected drains on your resources can damage the quality of your life. Protecting yourself from financial risks is a vital part of a good retirement plan. The way to do this is through insurance, and it's what we'll look at in the next chapter.

The One-Dollar iPhone

INSURANCE: REDUCING THE RISK IN YOUR FINANCIAL FUTURE

One day, while I was at work, I received a call from my wife, Wendy. She was at the cell phone store, where she had just purchased a previous-generation iPhone for the princely sum of $1. She wanted to know whether she should take up the salesperson's offer of phone insurance, at a cost of $60.

"Why would you pay $60 for insurance on a phone that's only worth $1?" I asked my wife.

"The salesperson told me that the phone is a $200 value," she replied, "so it makes sense to spend $60 per year on the insurance."

"Even if it was a $200 phone," I said, "if you pay $60 a year for insurance, after two years you will have paid more than half the phone's value over again. Paying $120 over two years on a $1 phone makes even less sense."

"The salesperson says it's worth $200," she repeated.

"No, it's worth $1. They're selling it for $1, so it's worth $1. He wants you to pay $60 a year on a $1 phone."

With that, my wife agreed that paying $60 for insurance on her new iPhone wasn't a good move, and we concluded the conversation.

Why am I telling you this? Because it illustrates an essential point about insurance. It makes no sense to pay large premiums to insure things that aren't particularly valuable. Many people don't know how to make this distinction, with the result that they overpay for insurance that they don't need. Some types of insurance are essential, but many are not.

Insurance may appear complicated, but it's actually very simple. It's a way to shift risk from you as an individual to an insurance company. When you pay a premium to an insurance company, you are paying them to take on risk for you.

Why is this important? First, it protects the asset you

choose to insure. If your house burns down, for example, your insurance company will cover the cost of replacing it. You pay a small amount of money, perhaps $2,000 to $3,000 a year, to insure your $500,000 home. In exchange, you have the peace of mind of knowing that your insurance company has assumed the risk of a major loss. A second scenario in which insurance is a good idea is when it will cover emergencies or unexpected expenses, such as the sudden death of a household income earner. This is, of course, called life insurance.

There are three factors to evaluate whether insurance is worthwhile: the degree of risk, the exposure to the risk, and the cost or premium for the insurance. You should always consider insurance in light of these factors. In the iPhone story recounted above, the cost of the insurance was more than the value of the asset, so the cost of insurance was way too high. What would you do if you lost or broke a one-dollar phone? Buy a new one.

Some people believe that all insurance companies are evil. That's a fallacy. In a free-market economy, we can always stop doing business with a particular insurance company and move to another one. This system creates natural competition that keeps prices down and motivates companies to give good service. Without competition, prices go up and monopolies form, which usually results in the government intervening to set prices, break up the companies, or worse yet, get involved in the business with additional regulation. This is evidenced by the track record of the government's history of getting involved in business, which doesn't work.

When you're deciding whether to take out insurance, you need to conduct a cost-benefit analysis. If your exposure to risk is high, it may be worth paying a high price to protect yourself. On the other hand, if your exposure to risk is moderate or low, it may not be worth paying very much at all to purchase insurance.

Let's look at the example of extended warranties. Most of these make no sense at all from a cost-benefit perspective. Televisions and other electronic equipment have become so cheap that the cost of the warranty, over the course of two or three years, can be almost as much as purchasing a new television.

Credit insurance—for example, financing a car, then purchasing insurance from the same company—rarely makes sense. Nor does accidental death and dismemberment insurance. Most people who pay for accidental death and dismemberment insurance think it's a good value because it's cheap and pays out a lot of money in the event of a catastrophe, but because most deaths are due to illness, whether sudden or prolonged, and the chance of an insurance company paying a claim is so low, they rarely pay a claim.

THE MOST VALUABLE FORMS OF INSURANCE

I've highlighted some types of insurance that offer little value, but there are a few types of insurance that I recommend.

HOME AND AUTO INSURANCE

Let's start with insurance on property. One type is homeowner's or renter's insurance. Another is automobile insurance, which is mandatory in most states because it protects the other party in the event of an accident. Both of these types of insurance insure against realistic risks at an acceptable cost.

EXCESS LIABILITY INSURANCE

Most people should also consider something called umbrella insurance, which will pick up any slack in the event that you exceed the limits of your homeowner's or automobile insurance. If the maximum payout on your automobile insurance is $500,000, for example, but you're in an accident and the other party sues you and gets a judgment for $2 million, your umbrella policy will cover the extra $1.5 million. Without an umbrella policy, all your personal assets could be exposed to a judgment in that scenario.

Now let's move on to insurance that covers you.

LIFE INSURANCE

Some years ago, my wife and I had young children and a mortgage on our first home. I was the main income earner in the family. Had I died unexpectedly, my wife would have been forced to sell the home. She would have been almost penniless, without enough money to raise and educate our children. Life insurance protected my earning power so that we knew my wife and young family would be safe in the event of my untimely death. If you care for people who would be negatively impacted without your income, you need life insurance.

DISABILITY INSURANCE

Perhaps more importantly, if you earn an income, you need disability insurance, because it pays out if you are unable to work due to illness or accident. For most people still in their working years, both life insurance and disability insurance are critical.

HEALTH INSURANCE AND MEDICARE SUPPLEMENT

As a recent or prospective retiree, you may also benefit from taking out a supplemental health insurance policy. As we discussed in the previous chapter, the potential costs of healthcare in retirement are frightening. According to the 2017 Fidelity Retiree Healthcare Cost Estimate,[*] a healthy sixty-five-year-old couple, over the course of their retirement, can expect to pay $275,000 in healthcare costs over their lifetime. By nature, such expenses are largely unpredictable, so there's no guarantee you won't spend even more than that. Even for people who are relatively wealthy, medical expenses can have a catastrophic impact on their finances.

Everyone in the United States receives Medicare coverage, but in some circumstances it proves inadequate. Even if you rely on Medicare, you should consider supplementing it with private insurance. This type of insurance is called Medicare Supplement or Medicare Advantage.

Some people have additional private insurance through the company that used to employ them. If this is your situation, it's important that you examine the extent of your coverage to make sure you're neither over insured nor underinsured. You would also be wise to consider the

---

[*] "Health Care Costs for Retirees Rise to an Estimated $275,000 Fidelity Analysis Shows," Fidelity, August 24, 2017, www.fidelity.com/about-fidelity/employer-services/health-care-costs-for-retirees-rise.

cost of your private insurance, because it's rarely free and may not be the best value available to you.

Even if you are covered by Medicare and private insurance, there could be gaps in your coverage. For example, Medicare might pay for everything except your first $100 of medical expenses per day, and your private insurance might cover only the first $50 per day. That leaves a shortfall of $50, which can quickly turn into $1,500 per month or even $18,000 per year. You may decide—preferably after consulting an expert in Medicare insurance—that the overall risks and benefits don't justify filling that hole. Even if that's the case, however, you should investigate thoroughly so you know what to expect.

LONG-TERM CARE INSURANCE

Another type of insurance that is very important as a retiree is long-term care insurance. This can protect you if you or your spouse need long-term in-home care, or if you need to live in a nursing home. With the exception of the first hundred days of care (and this isn't always the case), these expenses aren't covered by Medicare.

Many people think long-term care insurance is far too expensive, but there's a reason it's expensive—because there's a high probability that people who take out a policy will make a claim during their retirement. According to some statistics, 70 percent of adults over sixty-five will need long-term care during retirement.* When you take out long-term care insurance, you are shifting risk to your insurance company. Because the risk is very high, they must charge a high price.

Long-term care insurance may be expensive, but without it, the cost of long-term care can be crippling. With people living longer than ever, the chances that you will need in-home or nursing-home care at some stage in your life are considerable. A word of caution: there's some confusion over precisely what long-term care insurance covers, so make sure you check the fine print.

It's worth noting that long-term care can be an emotionally charged issue. For most people, the possibility of long-term care has negative connotations. They may feel that they would never want to live in a nursing home, or that they would never want a loved one to live in a nursing home. Some people even feel that they would rather die than subject themselves to a long-term stay in a nursing home.

There are new types of long-term care insurance where you get your money back if you don't ever use the insur-

---

* Richard W. Johnson and Gordon B. T. Mermin, "Long-Term Care and Lifetime Earnings: Assessing the Potential to Pay," The Urban Institute, US Department of Health and Human Services, August 2008, https://aspe.hhs.gov/basic-report/long-term-care-and-lifetime-earnings-assessing-potential-pay.

ance. This has made insuring against long-term care much more compelling.

The most important consideration is planning ahead. You may decide not to buy long-term care insurance, but you should make that decision consciously, in full understanding of the implications. In this area particularly, it's important to work with a financial advisor who is an expert—or can access experts—to evaluate your risk and analyze specific insurance plans.

ANNUITIES ARE INSURANCE

Some so-called experts caution people against taking out annuities. Others strongly recommend them. Dogmatism on either side of the argument can be a warning sign that all is not what it seems. Often, the people voicing strong opinions for or against annuities have a vested interest in their position. In this section, I'll break down what annuities are and explain their advantages and disadvantages.

Again, if you take out an annuity, you enter into a contract with an insurance company that protects you against losing your principal or living so long that you outlive your money. Some people claim that annuities are highly complex. That can seem to be the case, but actually, only the details are complicated. The principle is simple.

Should you choose to purchase an annuity, you are shifting two main risks to an insurance company. The first risk is outliving your money. In certain types of annuities, the insurance company is contracted to send you annual payments for as long as you live. It's similar to buying your own private pension.

The second risk—covered by a different type of annuity—is losing some of your principal during a stock market downturn. My family and I own in this type of annuity. It doesn't pay us a pension for the rest of our lives, although we could turn that benefit on in the future. Instead, it protects our money from adverse market conditions. If the market goes up, we receive some of the benefits from that gain. If the market goes down, we are protected from losses.

The advantage of annuities is that they offer a high level of certainty if properly used. By purchasing an annuity, you can generate an income for life, which can even—under specific contractual provisions—apply to your spouse in the event of your death. The income can even increase with inflation. Even if the total amount of money you receive from an insurance company exceeds the amount you spent on purchasing the original contract, you won't outlive annuity payments.

For this reason, some large companies use annuities as

contracts to pay out their pension obligations. They pay a lump sum to an insurance company in exchange for a contract that pays ex-employees an agreed amount every month for the rest of their lives. If annuities are so bad, why do many of the *Fortune* 500 companies buy them?

The downside of annuities is that you are either paying a fee directly for some of the benefits, or you are making a time commitment with a portion of your money. Remember that there is a significant risk you are shifting to an insurance company. One more thing: I believe most people should avoid variable annuities in a low-interest environment. The benefits just aren't good enough to justify the fees you are paying.

Putting some of your money into an annuity can be a wise move, depending on your unique situation, especially if you want to remove stock market risk from a portion of your portfolio. If you're considering one, I suggest speaking to a good financial advisor who is a fiduciary to help you to evaluate whether any type of annuity makes sense for you.

MAXIMIZING THE VALUE OF LIFE INSURANCE

We've already discussed how important it is to have some form of life insurance. In this section, I want to compare different types of life insurance in more detail. Nonetheless, it's important to understand that it's extremely difficult to make specific recommendations in the context of a book. Without knowing your specific situation, all I can do is explain how various forms of life insurance work and when they may be appropriate.

In my case, for example, I have altered my coverage over the years. As my income has increased, I have also increased the amount of life insurance I carry in order to protect the value of my future income for my family. I also have deposited my personal life insurance into a trust to protect it against estate taxes and any creditors.

As you approach retirement, it's a good idea to reevaluate your life insurance. As a general rule, the more money you have, the more worthwhile it is to include some degree of life insurance in your overall financial and estate-planning portfolio. For example, my father and I both have insurance planning in place, but no future premium payments are required. Our insurance will remain in force until we die, and if we want to, we can turn the cash value into pension payments that will last for the rest of our lives.

One thing to keep in mind is that life insurance is a tool to take care of (a) people you love, or (b) people you are obligated to, such as banks, mortgage companies, and so on.

As with every other form of insurance, it's important to

consider your life insurance needs carefully. If you're married, you will want to protect your spouse from a potential loss of income in retirement should something happen to you. They may be at risk of losing your Social Security check, and they could even see your pension reduced or terminated in the event of your death. You may also want to bequeath money to your kids or grandkids, especially if one of them has a special need, such as a disability. Life insurance can be a highly effective way of doing this.

Another way to use life insurance is to put it toward paying off debt, should you die owing money. If your estate is large enough to be eligible, life insurance can also cover estate taxes levied by the state or federal government. For these reasons, many wealthy families in the United States maintain a large amount of life insurance well into retirement.

As a business owner, I could use life insurance to equalize my estate. What does this mean? Imagine that I decide to pass my business—hypothetically valued at $1 million—to one of my four sons. In this scenario, one son would inherit the business, while the other three would receive an equal dividend—$1 million each—through life insurance. Of course, it's difficult or impossible to place an exact value on a business. An estimate, for the purpose of getting close to equalization, is fine. This approach allows me to be fair to all my children and prevents a situation arising in which one son receives a benefit and the others do not.

As you can see, insurance is a complicated subject, both in practical and personal terms. Often, we are influenced by feelings of insecurity; fears of illness, aging, and death; or even anxiety about losing a loved one. Insurance touches the depths of our relationships with others.

Due to these complexities, many people shy away from the subject altogether. That's understandable, but it's not the best way to proceed. We're all going to die. It's much wiser to address the issue directly, preferably with the assistance of a CERTIFIED FINANCIAL PLANNER™ professional or insurance expert who understands all of the available options and industry jargon. The answer to the question of whether you should own insurance depends on the risk, your exposure, and the projected value of the coverage, subjects that are best explored in detail with a professional. Remember, the key is to find someone whom you trust to always act in your best interest and to recommend only what is appropriate for you and your family.

In the next chapter, we'll discuss a range of tools and strategies you can employ to meet your retirement dreams, along with some of the risks you should be aware of. It's quite a technical chapter, but it will provide you with a framework for making investment decisions and asking the right questions of your financial advisor.

I Lost 90 Percent
of My IRA!

INVESTMENT TOOLS AND STRATEGIES

In the year 2000, I moved all my retirement money to tech stocks such as Microsoft, Cisco Systems, and Dell. Over the previous ten years, the broad market had averaged over 14 percent per year, with technology stocks performing much better than that. Over the following two years, those investments dropped 90 percent. It was a painful lesson, and it took me a long time to recover from the loss. In 2000, I was thirty-eight. Fortunately, I had many years to recover from that mistake. As a retiree, or someone who is planning to retire soon, you can't afford that time, which is why you need to think carefully about the level of risk you take. It took the NASDAQ (mostly technology) stock market index fifteen years to recover. You can't wait that long.

In this chapter, we will dig into the options you have for investing and, maybe more importantly, the real threats to your success.

Investments are the backbone of most plans. Their main purpose is simple: to provide a sustainable income for the duration of retirement. When you choose to invest your money, it should be with a focus on supporting the lifestyle you desire and deserve.

There are numerous ways to invest, including stocks, bonds, real estate, and partnerships. Like most financial products, each one has unique advantages and disadvantages. In this chapter, we'll examine their purpose and consider their applicability. The investment vehicles you choose in your thirties will almost certainly be different from the ones that serve you best in your fifties and sixties, so it's important to understand what will work best for you in retirement. When I was in my early thirties, I invested solely for growth. My primary goal was to achieve as much growth as possible. I wasn't investing for income.

Investing for growth can be risky. I learned about stock options and thought, foolishly, that this gave me an edge over the rest of the investing world. I promptly lost all the money I put into options—a hard lesson. Here's a good rule of thumb. When you, as an investor, think you have figured out something in the market that others have missed, you're playing a dangerous game. Most likely, you are wrong. Eventually, I learned to be cautious about getting involved in short-term trends and to follow a more tried-and-true approach.

As I go through my fifties, I have a very different attitude toward investment. When you consider investing later in life, your priorities should shift. In your thirties and forties, you were striving for maximum growth and accumulation. In your fifties and beyond, your priorities should be protecting your capital from a large downturn and receiving a reasonable rate of return. It's important to "smooth out your returns" because in retirement, you will no longer have the earning power to set money aside. You will need to preserve your existing principal so that it provides a solid, reliable return.

What sorts of investments should you use? In reality, there are many different types of investments. Most people, however, think primarily about the stock market or mutual funds, so we'll discuss those first.

THE STOCK MARKET

The stock market offers both big risks and big rewards,

which is why people are drawn to it, as I mentioned earlier. In the years leading up to 2000, when I worked in a financial securities business, stock market returns were absolutely spectacular. Almost every stock went up. I should have known there was danger ahead when I observed the cleaning person in our office giving stock tips to financial advisors. When everyone, even those with zero expertise, is making money, that's a good reason to be cautious.

Strange as it may sound, the biggest investment risk you face is your behavior. No one likes to think of themselves as greedy or fearful, but those impulses can have a major impact on our investing choices. This is why many people buy near the top of a market. They see a chance to make money, and they're afraid they'll miss out. What happens? Usually, the market goes down, they panic, and they end up selling close to the bottom. Many investors repeat this pattern time after time, buying high and selling low, until they've lost a significant amount of the money they had set aside for their future.

In a twenty-four-hour news cycle, we are constantly exposed to journalists and media personalities presenting questionable investment advice. Many of these media personalities are actually entertainers, so their true job is to keep people watching or listening to their program.

It's much easier to do that with a startling headline than with real, long-term advice.

Any investment recommendation needs to be considered in light of your own individual circumstances. These include your projected need for cash at a specific time in the future, your propensity to act on emotion, and how long it will be until you need the money. Given the volatile nature of the stock market, some surprises are unavoidable, but a strong financial plan built on sound advice will minimize the impact of those surprises.

Overall, it's a good idea to think of your investing life in two phases. During the early years of your career, you will want to build up your assets, then you will want to spend the second half of your career protecting those assets and generating income if needed. Even if you didn't need income, the idea is to smooth out the returns so you avoid the big downturns. A friend of mine did a quick analysis of all the annual market returns. He removed all years where the market lost more than 5 percent, and he removed all the years where the market made more than 15 percent. By doing this, giving up some upside and limiting the downside, he statistically has a better chance for success. He likes to say success lives between 5 percent and 15 percent. First build the nest egg, then protect the nest egg. For most of your career, you should save as much as you can and invest for growth—hopefully more wisely than I did when I learned about stock options. When you come within ten years of retirement, start to protect that nest egg and generate a reasonable rate of return by shifting to solid, lower-risk investments and products.

COMMON MISCONCEPTIONS ABOUT INVESTING

Along with the accumulated noise of a twenty-four-hour news cycle, we also filter our beliefs about investing through our own subconscious bias. The outlook we have developed through our upbringing, losses or wins we've experienced in the past, and maybe even concerns about loved ones naturally shape the way we interpret data.

These experiences become the building blocks of our preconceptions and misconceptions. For example, some people believe that the market always comes back, so they should simply buy stocks and hold them. In light of what we discussed in the previous section, this may seem like good advice. Indeed, it can be. However, it's important to take your own personal situation into account. If you need money while the market is down, you will be forced to sell at a loss. In this scenario, it doesn't matter whether the market always comes back. What matters is the state of the market when you need to sell. The money you take out never has a chance to recover.

Additionally, investing heavily in one or two stocks can have unexpected negative consequences. Following the banking crisis of 2008, for example, it took years for stocks to return to previous levels. If you had needed money for your retirement while the market was low, you would have taken a heavy hit when you liquidated those stocks or mutual funds.

Another common belief is that index funds, exchange-traded funds, or mutual funds counteract the natural risks of picking stocks. Each of these products is essentially a basket of different stocks. The advantage is that they provide buyers with a diverse range of stocks. By buying into one exchange-traded fund, QQQ for example, I can own stock in the top hundred companies in the NASDAQ with a single purchase.

Index funds can be great tools. On the other hand, they also carry a significant risk. What happens when a particular sector in the market turns down or, in the case of an S&P 500 fund, the entire market turns down? You may find that all of your stocks drop suddenly in value, or worse yet, they drop over months, triggering regret and feelings of "I should have just sold back in _____."

Nonetheless, some people believe that if they conduct their own analysis and examine the best-performing funds, they can emulate the success of investors. This may not be the case. If you purchase funds that have performed well over the last three to five years, you risk exposing yourself to excessive risk, because these trends don't tend to last. You may be buying future underperformance because many investment styles work in cycles. Something that was up for five years can underperform over the next five years.

The reason all of these misconceptions are so pervasive is that they all contain a degree of truth. Historically, it's true that the market always comes back, but not all investors are in a position to hold when the market takes a major downturn. It is possible that you could analyze the market yourself and make some good decisions. The problem is that without the experience of a professional, you may also make some costly decisions. You have a limited number of years to prepare for retirement, so you can't afford to take on the same level of risk as you would earlier in life. In short, all of these misconceptions contain some truth, but none are reliable enough to be used as guiding principles. Remember, it is your behavior that represents the biggest risk to you. A good financial advisor can get you to do things that are uncomfortable but get the best result (just like a coach understands that short-term pain can equal long-term gain).

STRATEGIES THAT WORK

With so many misconceptions, it may seem as though nothing is certain. Don't get discouraged, however. There are some tried-and-true strategies you can utilize.

One of the most effective is known as dollar-cost averaging. This is a strategy to take the emotion out of investing and deliver stable returns. It works by transferring a specified amount of money into a particular investment every month. If the market goes down, the same amount of money will buy a relatively higher number of shares. When the market goes up, that money will purchase fewer shares. When you do this, your average cost per share tends to decrease. Instead of chasing the market when it's high, you select a solid investment and purchase regularly. This is why for many people their 401(k) becomes a large retirement asset while they're not necessarily spending a lot of time and energy thinking about it.

This strategy addresses one of the greatest temptations investors face: attempting to buy into the market just before it rises and sell before it falls. This sounds good, but it's incredibly risky and difficult. Personally, I know of only three people who have succeeded long-term in predicting the ups and downs of the market, and very few people reading this book will be able to afford the high minimum costs.

When you are taking monthly income off a portfolio, dollar-cost averaging hurts you. You have to sell more shares when the market is down to generate that monthly check, and fewer shares when the market is up to generate that check. This is the opposite of dollar-cost averaging. You are selling fewer shares when the market is up and more shares when the market is down. This is why it is so important to have some of your money in products that will not lose value.

The fact that only a few money managers out of thousands have succeeded in this approach should clue you in to the fact that it's not a strategy to try for yourself, especially close to retirement. At this time in your life, you don't want the risk or exposure of trying to time the market. The only advice I can give you in this area is simple: don't do it.

Another powerful strategy is diversification. Usually, this involves investing in a variety of different assets, such as stocks, bonds, and real estate, although it's also possible to diversify within specific categories. For example, you could own a mutual fund with a hundred different stocks, or you could personally select a hundred different stocks instead of betting on a small number of them. You have heard the saying, "Don't put all your eggs in one basket."

Another classic way to reduce your risk over time is to

rebalance your investment portfolio. If some of your investments do much better than others, then, from time to time, you can sell some of the best-performing investments and reallocate those funds into investments that may not have performed well, but you believe will perform well in the future. Historically, this strategy has reduced risk by ensuring that investors sell high and buy low. It's best to do this at predetermined intervals. We rebalance our client portfolios regularly.

OTHER TYPES OF INVESTMENT

Discussing other investment strategies in depth is beyond the scope of this book, but let's briefly look at a few alternatives. The first is real estate, which means buying into a real estate fund or owning a piece of property. When you buy into a fund like this, you are indirectly investing in real estate. For example, you could buy a mutual fund that owns a hundred different real estate investments.

A more direct investment might involve purchasing individual rental properties, such as an office building, apartment building, or maybe a three-family home, and collecting the rent. This strategy naturally generates income and is attractive over the long term because it's naturally a hedge against inflation. Historically, real estate has always risen in value, so it's perceived as a strong investment. Assuming this continues, you will be able to raise the rent every few years, giving you a steadily increasing income as the value of the asset grows and rents rise. From a financial planning perspective, this is an excellent model.

It's important to stress that your own home is *not* a real estate investment. You need to live somewhere, so it should not be viewed as an investment.

Earlier, we talked about annuities and life insurance, both of which can make up part of a balanced investment portfolio. Certain types of annuities and life insurance are variable, which means they are considered securities. However, most of the annuities and life insurance we recommend at Johnson Brunetti are fixed insurance products with no stock market exposure on the downside. The insurance company guarantees your principal and the interest you have earned. You can't go backward.

You could invest in partnerships, either purchased through a broker or privately in collaboration with friends. These may offer high yields, but they are also risky and lacking liquidity. If you want to exit a partnership, you may pay a heavy price. With very few exceptions, I do not like these for our clients.

A final category of investment is the hedge fund. The term "hedge fund" is a broadly used phrase, and many so-called hedge funds don't actually hedge against the downside of the market. A more appropriate term to describe what they do would be "private investment partnerships." These may cover a diverse range of stocks, or they may focus on a specific area, such as tech stocks or companies the hedge fund manager feels are overvalued. It's worth remembering that most hedge funds are only available to investors with a high net worth and a great deal of money to invest. Many experts, including Warren Buffett, believe that hedge funds just don't provide good value.

NAVIGATING THROUGH THE CONFUSION

This book isn't a detailed investment guide, and it would be impossible to cover in depth all the possible investment options available to you. Nonetheless, I hope this chapter has familiarized you with the different investment tools and strategies at your disposal. With dozens of so-called experts sharing their opinions, many people are confused about the different types of investments and their value. By explaining how they work, I trust you'll have a general idea of which ones will suit you best, which should provide you with some clarity as you make your own investment decisions.

As with most topics discussed in this book, the best way to select investments is to consult a skilled and experienced financial planner whom you trust. In the next chapter, we'll tackle another subject of key importance to any retiree: estate planning.

The IRS and the Miami Dolphins

WHAT IS ESTATE PLANNING?

Have you ever heard of Joe Robbie? If you're thinking Joe Robbie Stadium, where the Miami Dolphins played, that's him. He owned the football team. When he died, the family had to sell the Miami Dolphins to pay estate taxes. This could have been avoided.

For many people, the concept of estate planning doesn't go beyond minimizing estate taxes. They come to us with the intention to protect their assets and reduce the probate fees they will pay when they pass on their estate to their heirs.

When we approach estate planning, however, we encourage clients to focus on their legacy. We want them to think about how they can turn their life's work into an expression of the people and things they care about deeply so that they leave a legacy that clearly reflects who they are.

Our estate is our life legacy. It's everything we leave behind, both material and immaterial, and our financial legacy is woven throughout it. The way clients plan their estates will inevitably reflect the feelings they have toward the people in their lives and their concerns about how the money they leave behind will be used.

Estate planning is a personal subject. Sometimes it creates friction because the client may feel a sense of guilt or obligation. For example, they may feel pressured to make decisions about their estate based on family entanglements, not based on who they are and the legacy they wish to leave.

PRACTICAL ESTATE PLANNING

Sometimes, people think of estate planning in extremely narrow terms. They imagine that it's all about tax planning or creating a will. In reality, there are three basic components of good estate planning. First is *asset protection*. Second is the *minimization of taxes and fees* at death. Third is *control* of how money and assets are used after death.

Some people invest for maximum income while alive, even if that means they spend the money down to zero by the time they die. Others wish to preserve their assets and perhaps limit their income, so that they can leave behind a large estate. Neither philosophy is right or wrong. It's a personal decision.

From a legal standpoint, attorneys can draft estate-planning documents to fulfill all kinds of dreams and address all kinds of fears. The trouble is that many attorneys do not ask the deep questions that are necessary to discover their clients' true priorities. This is where an expert in estate planning can help. As financial planners, we can't draft legal documents. However, we do advise clients on the many strategies they can use to accomplish their dreams. We also maintain referral partnerships with attorneys who fulfill the strategies we design.

Let's go through the three areas of asset protection, tax minimization, and control.

ASSET PROTECTION

What is asset protection? Most people think that it is about preserving their money in case of a long-term health problem, such as a stay in a nursing home or an extended spell of in-home care. This situation does likely present the highest risk to your assets. Normal medical insurance doesn't cover long-term health insurance, so you may need to buy an additional policy if you wish to protect yourself against the costs of long-term healthcare.

Alternatively, you could set up a trust and take the assets out of your name. For example, you could put your home into a trust so that you no longer technically own it. If you do this, enough time goes by, and you subsequently require long-term healthcare, Medicaid will pick up the costs. Medicaid is designed for people without assets, so you will need either to give away or spend everything you have before it will pay the bills. These techniques are complicated, and there is always a trade-off.

Again, you could protect your assets by gifting them into an irrevocable trust—you can spend all the money that remains in your name, and the Medicaid program will pick up your nursing-home expenses as long as certain rules and requirements are met. Long-term healthcare planning is only one element of asset protection, however. The other key component is putting in place protections against lawsuits or judgments.

Unlikely as it may sound, imagine that you accidentally crash into a school bus full of children, causing multiple injuries. In this case, you might be subject to a legal judgment far exceeding the limits of your insurance. Suppose you have half a million dollars of automobile insurance, and the judgment against you comes to $2.5 million. What happens to your retirement assets? Two million dollars of your personal assets are taken in the judgment. You need enough insurance to protect your assets so that they won't be garnished if there's a legal judgment against you.

This is where an umbrella policy can help. If your automobile insurance policy covers you for half a million dollars, you could purchase an additional umbrella policy for $2 million. Should your liability exceed half a million dollars, your umbrella policy will kick in and provide you with an additional $2 million in protection. Premiums for umbrella policies are low, so they can be an excellent option.

Personally, I have a $5 million umbrella policy to protect me in case I get in an accident or someone sues me. My wife and I purchased the coverage when our sons were teenagers. With two teenage drivers in the house, the chances of someone in the family having an accident increased. Whenever they drove my vehicle, I was exposed to that liability, so I protected myself.

Some people hold the mistaken idea that if they set up a joint bank account with their children, that account will be protected. This is not true. If you have a joint account with right of survivorship, then everything in the account is viewed, from a legal standpoint, as belonging 100 percent to every person whose name is on the account. It's not protected from liability. Furthermore, if you put your child's name on your account and they go through divorce proceedings, the money in your account is at risk. The only thing joint ownership does is facilitate efficient transfer of the account at death.

REDUCING TAXES AND FEES

Depending on your state of residence, probate fees and transfer costs can range from extremely low to extremely high. To minimize them, you need to work with a financial expert who understands the state in which you are a legal resident, along with any state in which you own property.

As of the writing of this book, federal estate tax applies only to assets above $11 million. Each spouse receives an $11 million exemption. Because of this, most people won't be exposed to federal estate taxes.

Nevertheless, your estate could be reduced by taxes before your loved ones get any assets. In the state of Connecticut, for example, in 2019, any money you bequeath to your children above $3.6 million is subject to taxation, paid prior to the transfer of property. Some people believe that if they inherit money from their parents, they will need to pay taxes, but that's not how it works. Taxes are taken care of in the estate settlement, and heirs receive the net. In Massachusetts, if your estate is over $1 million, the inheritance tax applies from the first dollar.

You'll want to coordinate your estate planning with federal laws, in the state where you live and in any state where you own assets. This will help you to minimize taxes and fees. With the help of skilled attorneys and financial planners, many people can reduce taxes or even eliminate them completely.

CONTROLLING YOUR MONEY

If you're a parent with children who are married, you have probably asked the question, "What if I leave money to my child and then they get divorced?"

People wish to control the way their money can be used after they die. They want their children to spend their money responsibly. Alternatively, they may feel hurt by the way a child or grandchild has treated them. Every family, like every organization, has its own politics. There are loyalties, rivalries, and emotional ties that must be addressed during estate planning.

Here's a personal example. I've done very well in life, while my brother has struggled to get ahead financially. He has done worthy work and lived responsibly, but he hasn't built much wealth. In my estate planning, after

I've taken care of my spouse and given my kids enough to help them but not enough to spoil them, I may want to set up a trust arrangement to take care of my brother and his family.

Perhaps there are people in your life to whom you want to exercise special benevolence. Maybe you admire the work they're doing, or you've seen them go through bad breaks, and you feel they deserve some compensation. You may want their kids to have the chance to get a great education. Good estate planning can enable you to do this.

CARE AND HOUSING OF SPOUSE AND PARENTS

I'm in my fifties. If I were to die unexpectedly, I would leave behind two elderly parents; a spouse; four children, three of whom are either in college or freshly out of college; and several businesses where I have controlling interests. How can I look after my parents, both financially and in terms of their health, while also taking care of my spouse and making sure I don't, in the process, disinherit my children?

In the United States, this situation is increasingly common. Earlier, we spoke about the sandwich generation, consisting of people who are currently aged between fifty and sixty. Members of the sandwich generation may have both elderly parents and children in their teens or twenties. Thirty years ago, this situation was incredibly uncommon because it was unusual for people to live well into their eighties. The parents of a typical fifty-year-old had already died by the time that person approached retirement. With advances in medicine, nutrition, and physical fitness, this has changed. Unfortunately, many people in the older generation didn't expect to live well into their ninth decade, so they are unprepared to support themselves.

I am part of the sandwich generation and will be for the next ten or so years. Naturally, I want to make sure that my spouse is provided for in the case of my death. Wendy, my wife, is fantastic at managing the home finances and spends money intelligently, but she doesn't know a lot about investments, so I need to have a "post-death" plan in place.

In the past, this was a common dynamic. The husband usually handled investments while the wife ran the home. Nowadays, however, we often see these roles reversed. Right now, for example, we're working with a woman who is a high-level executive at a chemical company. Her husband is a carpenter and home remodeler. She runs all of the finances, so she needs to make sure her husband will be taken care of if something happens to her.

In case I die before my wife, I have prepared a list of

people I want her to consult for financial advice, because I don't want her to make those decisions in a vacuum. Unless she has access to good advice, she's unlikely to make changes to our investment portfolio. This would likely be a mistake, because her altered situation would call for an altered approach to managing her investments.

Unless I specify to whom she should turn, there's also a risk that she will consult people who won't act in her best interest, meaning that she will receive bad advice or poor financial management. As part of my estate planning, I want to direct her to a financial advisor I already trust.

My personal circumstances illustrate one possible estate-planning scenario. There are many others. Many families include individuals with disabilities—physical or mental—who require care and medicine, for example. In some cases, one member of a family struggles with alcohol or substance abuse. In such cases, we want to take care of people while simultaneously protecting them from poor financial decisions.

YOU CAN CONTROL FROM THE GRAVE

Many people don't realize that they can exercise significant control over the way their money is spent long after they're dead by setting up trust documents. These can be used to attach conditions to inheritances, meaning that if someone behaves in a way incongruent with your values, you can restrict access to your money.

My wife and I have set up a trust that functions in this way. If our children were to behave in ways we deem unacceptable, our money could bypass them, be held in trust, and pass to our grandchildren. Not every rule attached to trusts is punitive, however. For example, you may wish to stipulate that if one of your children devotes their life to low-paid charitable work, they receive an additional stipend.

There are many ways to control the disbursement of funds long after you're gone. This is important because you may have children or grandchildren who behave wastefully or who are simply not practically minded. Alternatively, they might marry someone you distrust.

When I speak in public, I often ask my audience, "How many of you moms love your kids?" Of course, all the mothers in the room raise their hands, and everyone smiles. Then I say, "OK, how many of you moms still don't like the people your kids married?" People laugh, but it's a powerful example. You may trust your children to use your money wisely, but do you trust their spouses?

As alluded to earlier, a client might leave a million dollars to a son who is married with children but then stipulate that if their son dies, all of the money goes to the children. In case of a divorce, they may want half of their money to go to the son while the other half goes immediately to the children. This kind of flexibility assures clients that they can plan for and handle any changes that might affect their families in the future.

The key here is, if you have an idea or restriction you would like to put into place, write it down. It is likely that the right attorney can facilitate your wishes.

LEAVING LEGACY GIFTS

As we discussed in chapter 4, most people follow a similar set of priorities. Once they know they will be okay financially for the rest of their lives, they want to take care of their kids. Once they know that their kids and grandkids will be fine, their next move may be to make a significant contribution to charity.

The charity people choose is usually a highly personal decision. My wife's sister died from a form of blood cancer, so my wife strongly wants to donate money to the search for a cure. On the other hand, sometimes people base their choices on custom. For example, they might donate to the same church or synagogue as their parents did.

Two of the most common charities people donate to are the Alzheimer's Foundation of America and the American Cancer Society. A high percentage of people in the United States will deal with either cancer or a degenerative brain disorder as they age, so it's understandable that many people wish to support these organizations.

When your attorney does your document preparation for your estate plan, it should include a living will, powers of attorney, and medical directives. You need to appoint someone to speak on your behalf if you are alive but cannot do so.

As you can see from this chapter, estate planning is far more than the technical process of setting up a will and trust. It's a personal, emotional issue that differs greatly from family to family. It's essential that you work with the right financial, legal, and tax advisors to design your estate plan which accurately reflects your personal values.

In the final part of this book, we'll discuss specifically how to provide for your children and grandchildren in your will, and how to share your hard-earned financial wisdom with them in a way they can relate to.

PART III

They Don't Need
to Go to Harvard

YOUR CHILDREN'S AND
GRANDCHILDREN'S FUTURE

My oldest son, Brandon, is in his late twenties and works as a service manager at an automotive shop in Boston. He loves cars and owns multiple cars and motorcycles. My second son, Michael, is a lieutenant in the Marine Corps, so he will be well remunerated as long as he serves. My third and fourth, Joel and Noah, are in college as I write this. As their father, I am hopeful about their future. That said, it is a different world today than the one I grew up in. Will they have the same opportunities that I did? Will they find work that pays them adequately?

As for me, despite attending schools of less than the highest quality, I managed to build a multimillion-dollar business that has helped thousands of families, but I don't want my experience to prejudice my attitudes toward my children. We've all heard about parents who pressure their children to follow a specific career trajectory. I don't want to be that type of father.

My son Noah's friend comes from a Pakistani family. In Pakistani culture, it is common for parents to limit the career choices of their children. His friend often jokes that he has two career options: doctor or engineer. Of course, this dynamic can occur in any family, and maybe it is a strength. I just have a different philosophy—not better, just different.

When parents push their children toward a specific career, it's usually due to their own experiences. In a family of doctors, children may feel pressure to become doctors, whether the pressure is really there or not. In a family of lawyers, there may be an underlying assumption that the children will become lawyers. Some of them, of course, may not want to become lawyers and instead dream of becoming social workers. Sometimes parents hope that their children will fulfill the parents' own unrealized dreams.

People who grew up in the sixties and seventies believed

that if they worked the same job for forty or fifty years, they would be well taken care of in their old age. In the twenty-first century, that idea seems to have disappeared, and no one knows for sure what the political, social, and economic landscape will look like when today's children reach retirement.

With all these competing factors, it's natural to feel anxiety about the future of the young people in your family. I encounter similar fears in many clients entering retirement. They worry, with some reason, that future generations will not experience the opportunities and prosperity that they enjoyed. Many people are motivated to help the younger generations.

THE COST OF COLLEGE

A client of mine, whom I'll call Bob, has made what looks to me like a serious mistake. Bob is five years away from retirement, but he has taken on $250,000 in debt to put his kids through expensive, elite East Coast schools. As a construction worker, Bob has a modest income and little money in retirement savings. In effect, he has impoverished himself and his spouse to send his kids to elite schools.

Bob will undoubtedly pay a very heavy financial price for his decision. In my opinion, he would have been wiser to send his kids to a good school such as the University of Massachusetts or the University of Connecticut. Those kids might not have received the "elite education" they would at Harvard or Yale, but they would still have received a leg up in life. Meanwhile, Bob and his wife, Joan, wouldn't be forced to sell their house and rent an apartment to pay off the debt.

I see situations like this frequently. People in the Northeast, for example, feel tremendous pressure to send their kids to expensive schools, which can create some serious financial issues. It also puts tremendous pressure on the kids themselves.

The larger point here is that if you choose to borrow against retirement, you could wind up broke and living with your highly educated kids. I am familiar with studies that say education is only a small part of one's overall success.

When you plan for your children, no doubt you want them to attend the best possible schools. Nonetheless, overreaching can be dangerous. You would be wise to ask yourself what you can honestly afford and what type of school is most appropriate for them. Ultimately, their own decisions and discipline will have at least as much of an impact on their success as the place they go to school.

My wife and I decided that we wanted our children to bear

some of the cost of their education. We could have paid 100 percent of our oldest son's education, but we wanted him to understand how it felt to invest in his future, so he took out some student loans. A few years after his graduation, when we were in a better financial position, I offered to pay off his student loans. He surprised me and made me very proud when he said he would rather pay them off himself.

My second son received a full scholarship from the military, but he had to earn it by maintaining his grades and physical fitness and by demonstrating leadership capabilities. He contributed to his own education by earning the scholarship. My third and fourth sons will also bear some of the cost of their university education. By doing this, we hope they will learn not only the subjects they study but also the principles of financial responsibility.

CONTRIBUTING TO COLLEGE

While I hope you won't invest so heavily in your children's education that you put yourself in a similar situation to Bob's, it's natural that you want to support your children— or even your grandchildren—as they gain an education. To do this, there are specific tools you can employ.

For example, a program called the 529 savings plan allows you to invest money for qualified educational expenses.

All the growth and gain can be withdrawn tax-free as long as it is used for education, housing, and other costs. Another option is Coverdell Education Savings Accounts, which work similarly but have lower limits. A third is government savings bonds. When these are taken out by a parent and used for college education, the parents are exempt from paying taxes on the interest, although this law could change.

In certain states, it's possible to invest in prepaid tuition programs. In the state of Michigan, I could invest a small amount into a prepaid tuition program when my child or grandchild is two years old. The state guarantees that no matter what the cost is by the time that child turns eighteen, it will cover tuition for an in-state school, such as the University of Michigan or Michigan State. You may consider using a Roth IRA to pay for college, because the money comes out tax-free, or if it's applicable to the circumstances of your children or grandchildren, investigating scholarship programs for military veterans or current members of the military.

Finally, if you can afford it, you may simply pay your child's or grandchild's tuition as they progress through college. You may do this by liquidating stocks, bonds, or mutual fund portfolios to pay for it, as long as you're still taking care of your own financial needs. There are limits to how much you can give to anyone other than your spouse without filing a gift tax return. Many attorneys are of the opinion, though, that if you pay directly for a child's or grandchild's college education, the money you spend doesn't count toward that limit.

As with every other subject in this book, you should investigate each of these tax-advantaged ways to save for college with the assistance of a financial planner.

PUT YOUR OWN OXYGEN MASK ON FIRST

When it comes to your children's or grandchildren's education, it's natural that you will want to help them as much as possible. Nonetheless, there are a couple of issues to bear in mind. First, please make sure that you plan for your financial future first so that you don't impoverish yourself to pay for their education. Second, understand that many people fear that their children and grandchildren won't have the same opportunities they had in life. These fears may be valid, but it's also true that many generations throughout history have felt the same way. Therefore, resist the temptation to make decisions out of fear or guilt, especially if it will hurt you financially.

In the final chapter of this book, we'll discuss one of the trickiest financial topics there is: talking to your children and grandchildren about money.

Why Do They Spend Money Like That?

TALKING WITH CHILDREN AND GRANDCHILDREN ABOUT MONEY

When I was twenty-seven, I started making decent money. I had loved cars since I was a kid and wanted to buy a nice Corvette. I found the perfect car and took out a seven-year loan to buy it—a financial decision I now realize was foolish. By the end of the seven years, the car was practically worthless. I've told my children that story, and they seemed to absorb it better than if I had simply told them not to finance a car over more than three or four years. There are many lessons we can teach our grandchildren about money.

Let's suppose that I'm a grandparent. I don't approve of the way my children spend money, and I doubt that my grandchildren are prepared to handle money responsibly. They're easily tempted by instant gratification, and they have no idea how to use financial products such as mortgages. I want to help them as much as possible. What can I do?

Maybe you can relate to the feeling. In this chapter, I want to offer you some smart ways to communicate with your children, and particularly grandchildren. You may find that your grandchildren will listen to you more readily than they will listen to their parents, which gives you a unique opportunity to exercise a positive influence.

Most of us, as we enter our fifties, sixties, and seventies, look back with regret at some of the financial decisions we made in our younger years. Maybe we purchased a vacation home that we didn't use as much as we had anticipated. Maybe we took out an unwise loan or bailed out someone who never repaid our trust.

In our experience, many clients worry that their children and grandchildren will make the same mistakes they did. It could be too late to influence your own children, especially if they're already in their mid-twenties, thirties, or forties. If that's the case, they've probably already developed their philosophy of life. However, you have powerful influence on your grandchildren. Their future remains wide open. You know what? They want your advice.

Will they have the knowledge to make good financial decisions? Are they frugal? Do they have basic common sense or street smarts? Do they exercise self-discipline, or do they bounce through life without considering their financial future?

I have a client with two kids who are very different from each other. The older one is twenty-nine, while the younger is twenty-one. Both are responsible, avoid taking on debt, and save money, but they have totally different relationships with money. Unless the older child inherits money or receives seed capital to start a business, it's unlikely he'll ever be wealthy. The younger child, on the other hand, is extremely sharp financially. I would bet the farm that he will become wealthy.

These different personalities will likely lead to different financial outcomes, but it's not a cause for concern. Before you attempt to communicate with your children and grandchildren about money, make sure that your concerns are grounded in reality. Make a distinction between natural variation between their personalities and worries based on a realistic assessment of their behavior and what's happening in the world.

HEALTHY FINANCIAL COMMUNICATION

Ultimately, you can't control the decisions of your children and grandchildren, but it's still your duty and right to advise them on those decisions. As a parent, I often find that my sons resist my advice due to their drive to achieve independence. They're often far more open to advice delivered by my father.

While it's hard for parents to talk to their children about money, it's not impossible. One of the best ways to overcome resistance is to tell personal stories instead of delivering lectures.

As tempting as it may be, resist the impulse to constantly give advice and lecture. Choose special moments and tell stories to drive home the lessons you wish to teach. Nothing conveys a lesson better than sharing personal pain. Always treat your children and grandchildren with respect. Instead of criticizing specific decisions they have made, share principles and guidelines they may find useful.

Suppose that my son purchases a stock and loses a lot of money. I could tell him he should never have bought the stock, but by this time, he probably knows this. Criticism will only cause him to feel bad or become defensive. Alternatively, I could approach him with curiosity and ask, "What was your thought process when you bought that stock, and what do you know now that you didn't know then?" By inviting him to think through his decision verbally, I'm encouraging him to see where he has made mistakes.

Finally, I could approach him by sharing a story about a poor stock decision I made and learned from in my past. Through my story, I can teach him always to do due diligence and not to jump to snap investment decisions, and he will be more willing to receive it.

Finally, be aware of your own filters and biases. If some emotional event in your past shapes your advice, be honest about it. Your children and grandchildren will make mistakes. It's okay. Everyone makes mistakes, and we learn from them. Long ago, I learned that I need to let go of the illusion that I can control every decision my kids make. My relationship with them is much more important than winning a particular battle. The more I treat them as mature adults, the more they will be open to my advice.

SPECIFIC ADVICE FOR YOUNG PEOPLE

Now that we've addressed emotions and how best to communicate financial advice to children and grandchildren, let's delve into some specific issues. First, we'll discuss two specific areas—spending and debt—where young people often struggle. Then we'll examine some basic saving principles.

As we discussed in chapter 1 of this book, self-knowledge is a large part of making good financial decisions. Do you make decisions based on emotion, or are you a logical thinker? You can discover this by looking at your interests. Engineers tend to be analytical, investigative thinkers, for example. Artists and athletes tend to base their decisions more on emotion. They tend to be impulsive.

Analytical people may become so caught up in analyzing every possible outcome that they become unable to make decisions. Emotional people, by contrast, may be prone to making decisions based largely on intuition. Both types benefit from stepping out of their comfort zone. For analytical types, this may mean forcing themselves to make a decision based on 80 percent of available information. For emotional types, it could mean disciplining themselves to collect enough data before they leap. To talk to the young people in your life successfully, understand their personality type.

SETTING UP A PROTECTIVE ENVIRONMENT

I always advise young people to surround themselves with others who complement their ways of thinking and to set up their financial environment to protect themselves from their worst impulses. Let me describe what I mean.

When I was younger, I had a checking account and a savings account. In those days, the only way to take money out of the savings account was to go to the bank, fill out a form, and hand it to a bank teller, at which point the money could be withdrawn in cash or transferred to my checking account. That environment placed a brake on my impulsive desire to remove money from my savings account. I had to think about the decision a little harder, then go down to the bank, which made it more likely that my money would remain in my savings account.

Nowadays, young people can immediately transfer money from savings to checking using their bank's iPhone app. This makes it much easier for young people to spend their money freely—perhaps too freely. At the other end of the scale, my father, who is eighty-two, didn't even own a credit card until he was in his thirties. In those days, impulsive spending was difficult. Now it's staggeringly easy.

My son Joel is in college. He has two bank accounts. One account has a debit card attached to it, but the other is a long-term savings account that he rarely touches. In order to withdraw money from the savings account, he has to transfer it to the debit card account. He can't remove the cash directly unless he goes into the bank. In his world, nobody goes into a bank. This makes it at least a little harder to spend impulsively from his savings account. It's the nearest equivalent to the way things were when I was young.

TALK ABOUT FORMING GOOD HABITS

When we do something ten or twenty times, it becomes easier to keep doing it. It's like driving a car down a dirt road. As we do it repeatedly, we start to create a rut. The deeper that rut becomes, the harder it is to get the car out. This is why it's a good idea to pay attention to the habits your children and grandchildren are forming.

I meet many people who borrow money to buy a new car every two or three years. They get into that habit and, after doing it a few times, continue doing it all the way to retirement. The opportunity cost of taking on so much debt is enormous: if they had instead bought cars that were two or three years old and driven them for seven or eight years, they could have invested thousands of extra dollars for their retirement.

Bad habits can lead to disaster, while good habits can result in more freedom. For many years now, my wife and I have saved between 15 and 25 percent of our income every month. We started doing that when my income first went up, and we've stuck with it. Now it's such a strong habit that we don't even think about it. We do it automatically.

To make that possible, we've avoided stretching our finances too thin. We haven't bought larger and larger houses just because we could, as so many people do. Instead, we chose to save the extra money. Whatever is left over, we can spend. We enjoy life. We take time off, go on trips, and have fun.

Enjoying life is important. My grandparents grew up in the Great Depression, and they often went without any luxuries because their families were afraid of going broke at any moment. As a result, they lived a life of strict self-discipline and frugality.

A business coach of mine likes to say, "In heaven, there's not going to be a reward for suffering through life." Depending on your religious beliefs, you may not agree, but I do believe we can all strive for a healthy balance between enjoying life and saving money. Have your grandchildren start with an emergency fund of perhaps two to six months' worth of expenses.

When you talk to your children and grandchildren, encourage them to form positive financial habits that will last them a lifetime, and gently discourage habits that will drain their resources.

You may want to tell your children and grandchildren that the average American has only $120,000 saved when they get to retirement. That means at the high end, some have a million or two million dollars, but at the other end, there are many who have nothing. To put this in perspective, $120,000 can create an income of about $500 a month in retirement. That's not a lot of money.

Because of this, they should always save 10 to 15 percent of their gross income. If they start doing this in their thirties, they will be prepared for retirement. All they need is a moderate rate of return—4, 5, or 6 percent. They don't need to hit any investment home runs, such as discovering the next Apple or Google stock. A moderate rate of return will put them in good shape for retirement.

If you suggest to a child or grandchild in their thirties that they start saving 10 to 15 percent of their income, they may be shocked. In our high-spending world, it will probably seem like a lot. It's hard for young people to save 10 to 15 percent, and they might experience some lean times when they can't do it. If that happens, encourage them to take every opportunity to make up for it.

In his book *The Automatic Millionaire*, my friend David Bach talks about making savings automatic. David's book is great for any young person who needs to learn the principles of saving first. I highly recommend it. Any money they want to save for use at least five years in the future should be put in a mutual fund, 401(k) plan, or possibly an S&P 500 index fund. They may be able to use a 401(k) or 403(b), where the money comes out of their paycheck automatically before they even see it and goes into an investment program.

Some people enjoy the security of having a budget. You can talk to your kids about creating a detailed budget. You might encourage them to carry a small notebook around and write down every expenditure they make. If a paper notebook seems dated, they can use a budgeting app on their phone. They will probably find that they spend far more on many items than they realize. For example, they might be surprised to discover that they spend $200 a month on Starbucks.

DEALING WITH DEBT

One of the most important things you can do for your children or grandchildren is to talk to them about the effects of debt. Help them understand that the short-term effect of borrowing is a loss of freedom, both practically and psychologically. This is because whenever we are in debt, we live with the knowledge that we owe some other entity a sum of money. It is an obligation, and we feel it.

Debt also impacts cash flow. When we borrow money,

we must at least pay the interest, if not the interest and principal. Sadly, it's not uncommon to see people in their thirties spending $700 to $1,000 a month on a car payment, which is a huge waste of money. There are also hidden costs to relationships: many couples argue about money, with many of those arguments centered on debt.

GOOD DEBT VERSUS BAD DEBT

In reality, there is a distinction between good debt and bad debt. Good debt involves borrowing money to invest in something that will probably increase in value, such as a home or an education. As we discussed earlier, some people spend too much on education, but borrowing to pay for a reasonably priced education in a field with historically good earning power could be a very sound investment.

Car loan = bad debt. Mortgage on a home = good debt.

You may wish to discuss the earning power of your grandchildren's chosen major. A degree in engineering, architecture, or medicine, for example, will probably offer a better financial return than a degree in gender studies. If they borrow $200,000 to pay for a degree that the market doesn't value, it will not be a good investment.

It's always a bad idea to borrow money to go on vacation,

buy a timeshare, buy furniture, or pay for anything that is sure to reduce in value. I learned this the hard way when I got into debt buying that brand-new Corvette.

There is a third category of debt: debt incurred to cover the costs of an emergency, such as a leaking roof or a broken furnace. Many people borrow money to pay for repairs when their insurance doesn't cover it, usually with a high-interest credit card. When water starts pouring through the roof, they have to get it fixed no matter what it costs, so they don't have a lot of choice.

To avoid borrowing to cover the costs of emergencies, everyone should create an emergency fund, and you may wish to advise your children or grandchildren to do so. I mentioned this earlier. An emergency fund should not be confused with long-term savings. It is a buffer for unexpected expenses. Again, an emergency fund should contain three months' worth of current spending: someone living on $3,000 a month should have $9,000 saved for emergencies.

You should be extremely careful about cosigning or guaranteeing a loan for a child or grandchild. If you, as a grandparent, step up and guarantee a home or car loan, you are putting yourself at risk. Should your grandchild default on the loan, you will be wholly responsible for paying it back.

Similarly, you must be cautious when bailing your kids out of debt. It's hard for a parent or grandparent to watch their child deal with the effects of a poor financial decision, but it could be one of the best lessons they learn in life. When asked to cosign or help your grandchildren out of debt, be cautious of your emotions. You might be encouraging irresponsible behavior or even lowering their self-esteem.

Ultimately, the decision is yours. If you're considering helping a child or grandchild with debt, remember to consider the financial impact on yourself. It's good to help others where possible, but you don't want to sacrifice your retirement lifestyle and possibly become impoverished simply because you pulled someone out of a difficult situation.

PASS ON YOUR WISDOM

In conclusion, you are in a unique position to communicate the financial lessons you've learned to your children and grandchildren. Teach them the principles you've learned that you maybe didn't understand when you were younger. Each generation stands on the shoulders of the previous generation, learning from their behavior and wisdom. Where possible, do this with stories and personal examples so they can relate to what you tell them and absorb the lessons for themselves.

Your grandchildren need to learn both positive lessons and negative lessons about money, and you can help them. Use the wisdom you have gained from your own mistakes to help them with their own financial future, while respecting their autonomy and desire for independence. If you're a grandparent, they are more likely to listen to you than to their parents. They look up to you, so you have their ear. Use it well.

Conclusion

This is my ninth book. This book is different from the others I have written. It captures years of wisdom I have learned from my parents, clients, and personal experiences. Most importantly, it explores the emotions, good and bad, around money.

Throughout this book, we've covered a lot of ground and explored many complicated and sensitive topics related to financial planning. We've discussed how feelings drive financial decisions as much as knowledge and pointed out the disconnect between the cookie-cutter advice offered by financial experts and the way people behave around money. When it comes to making wise financial decisions, knowledge isn't enough. We need the wisdom that comes from experience and self-understanding.

Both the practical and personal aspects of financial planning can be daunting, which is why many people are better off working with a skilled financial advisor. If you're looking for a financial advisor, choose one who knows and understands you, who isn't afraid to deliver a little tough love when you need it, and who can act as a coach to encourage you to do the right things. Unless your financial advisor understands your behavior and emotions, the best advice in the world will be of little value.

The good news is that planning for your future can be easier than many pundits suggest. Many people in the world of financial advice make things sound more complicated than they need to be to foster a sense of dependency. Sometimes good old-fashioned common sense will get you most of the way to a secure financial future. Nonetheless, it's important that you resist the urge to procrastinate. Securing your financial future requires you to take action. It won't sort itself out.

I've been helping people with money since 1989. Over the years, I've seen our company's mission statement become more and more applicable. Our goal is to take the fear out of your financial future and give you confidence in what lies ahead. That goal is attainable in your life, and I hope this book has provided you with both inspiration and practical advice to move you toward a more positive financial future.

About the Author

JOEL JOHNSON is a CERTIFIED FINANCIAL PLANNER™
professional who has worked in financial services since
1989, helping thousands of families develop individual-
ized retirement plans. He hosts a weekly financial radio
show, *Money Wisdom*, and financial segments on WCVB
Boston and WFSB Hartford for a program called *Better
Money*.* Joel is the author of several books, has written
for the *Wall Street Journal*, and is a monthly contributor
to *Forbes*.

Joel is a managing partner of Johnson Brunetti, a New
England-based retirement and specialty investment firm,

---

* The weekly financial shows for radio and the financial segments on television are
  paid sponsorships.

which supports numerous nonprofits, including the Salvation Army, Veterans Association of America, Wounded Warrior Project, Dress for Success, and Make-A-Wish®.